Birmingham...
The Sinister Side

CRIME AND THE CAUSES OF CRIME IN VICTORIAN AND EDWARDIAN TIMES

INTRODUCTION

During the reign of Queen Victoria the ratio of violent deaths occurring through crime in the 'city of the thousand trades' was higher than in any other part of the country. Altercations in the densely-populated slum-areas were inevitable.

Home for most Brummies was a couple of foul-smelling rooms where often whole families might share the same bed. Abject poverty, both financial and emotional, was the major factor in undermining family life. The children of depressed mothers quickly found themselves at odds with the law and harsh punishments served as little deterrent.

Life in all major industrial cities was harsh and the sole pleasure for many lay in the ubiquitous public house. Most of the murders and cases of assault were perpetrated on women by drunken men.

Built to help industry, the famous canals served both the murderous and suicidal in equal measure.

Brummie or visitor, join us in a trip back in time to experience the sights, smells and brutish facts of existence in what is now Britain's number two city.

Join us in Birmingham...the Sinister Side.

STEVE JONES, SEPTEMBER 1998

About the Author....

Since originally being published in 1998, Birmingham... The Sinister Side has sold over 30,000 copies and been re-printed several times. The author Steve Jones wrote 13 books in total, two of which were translated into Japanese and Chinese.

The late Dave Cross, curator of the West Midlands Police Museum, contributed heavily to the original Sinister Side book; assisting author Steve Jones with access to the police archives and prisoner mug shots.

In July 2018 the museum contacted Steve to ask if the book could be re-printed again, in order to get this fantastic book seen and enjoyed by more people, and to help raise funds for the museum. Steve agreed and was pleased that his book would once again be for sale. After visiting the Lock-up he was excited by the plans to relocate the museum and happy to support them.

Sadly Steve died suddenly of heart failure in August 2018, before the book was re-printed. He left behind a wife, Christina, and a 13-year-old son Tommy.
This book is therefore dedicated to the memory of the man who told the story of criminality in Victorian and Edwardian Birmingham so wonderfully, bringing history to life for so many people.

Steve Jones
29th June 1951 – 26th August 2018

First published in September 1998
Re-published by Mapseeker Digital Ltd
in association with the West Midlands Police Museum

Mapseeker Digital Ltd, Unit 15, Bridgwater Court,
Oldmixon Crescent, Weston Super Mare, North Somerset, BS24 9AY
Telephone +44 (0) 01922 458288 +44 (0) 7947107248

© **Steve Jones 1998**

ISBN 978-1-84491-886-7

This book is copyright. No part of it may be reproduced in any form without permission in writing from the publishers except by a reviewer who wishes to quote brief passages in connection with a review written for inclusion in a newspaper, magazine, radio or television broadcast.

By the same author:

LONDON...THE SINISTER SIDE

WICKED LONDON

THROUGH THE KEYHOLE

CAPITAL PUNISHMENTS

IN DARKEST LONDON

WHEN THE LIGHTS WENT DOWN

NOTTINGHAM...THE SINISTER SIDE

MANCHESTER...THE SINISTER SIDE

CONTENTS

1. **BRUM'S SLUMS** 4
   Contemporary accounts of the harsh struggle for existence

2. **'A WOMAN, A DOG AND A WALNUT TREE'** 16
   Brutish Brummies turn their self-loathing onto their wives

3. **THE VISITATION OF GOD** 29
   Children were in danger from pestilence, poverty and their parents

4. **BORN TO BE WILD** 38
   The young offenders who made both their own and others' lives hell

5. **'FRESH FROM BRAWLING COURTS'** 45
   Anarchy, violence, drama and humour – all human life was there

6. **'CAN YOU READ? CAN YOU WRITE? CAN YOU FIGHT?'** 64
   Tales from the Victorian boys in blue

7. **OUT OF SIGHT, OUT OF MIND?** 71
   The inhabitants of Winson Green Prison bid you 'welcome'

8. **THE LOVER, IN THE KITCHEN, WITH THE REVOLVER** 85
   The Victorian way of murder

9. **CANAL, CUT-THROAT OR CARBOLIC?** 97
   The dilemmas faced by the city's suicidal

BRUM'S SLUMS

1. Windsor Street. For many women life was one long round of child bearing and burying.

The official Birmingham 'Inspector of Nuisances', Mr. R Wooley, had an impossible job. In mid-Victorian times he was responsible for bringing cases against persons for *allowing nuisances to exist on their premises.* He probably didn't know where to start.

In those days, you could be fined for a range of offences such as having foul drains; foul ashpits; the keeping of pigs; failure to remove garbage after slaughtering and having diseased pork dressed for sale. Occasionally pigs, even horses shared the family home.

There lingered a perpetual stench in such areas as the Inkleys, where human refuse was stored in the house throughout the day, while at night:

> The door is opened, and it is thrown out without the least reference to the spot where it falls.

Effluent seeped through sandstone, polluting water supplies. Death rates in contaminated areas were two and a half times higher than in uninfected areas. One social commentator, aptly named White, captured the sights and smells of the slums of 1875. He described just how desperate conditions were for tens of thousands of inner city dwellers:

> The floors of the houses are damp, some of them are lower than the level of the courts, and some, as I have before described, suffer from the oozing of filth and nastiness through the walls, emitting horrible stenches; and battle with them as they may, the people seem utterly unable to remove the evils. The amount of sickness which is evidenced by the death-rate is enormous.
>
> On going from house to house we see another case, the fireside of the only sitting room had to be deserted, owing to the noxious percolation from a privy penetrating the wall within a foot or two of the easy chair.
>
> A house in which the little savings of an industrious man, £40, had been invested in the stock and goodwill of a greengrocery, was so frightfully leaky that, on being taken up into the back chamber, I found the ceiling had fallen down upon the children's bed, while the water had streamed through the bed on which the husband and wife slept, in the next floor, down into their only sitting room.
>
> Some of the worst houses are so small and low that it is a matter of wonder how such places can ever have been put up for human habitation. In one case I found a house of only two rooms, about nine feet square each, and 6 feet, 6 inches high; and in this hovel lived husband, wife and four children, the eldest between fifteen and sixteen. In others I have seen people ill with severe colds and bronchitis, and snow-water flowing down the stairs like a

cataract on the kitchen floor. In another the people left their beds in terror, seeking the shelter of a neighbouring house from falling tiles and chimney-pots.

Progress in this area of life was slow. Very little appeared to have changed a quarter of a century later, when a reporter visited deprived areas around the turn of the century:

Love Lane, Birmingham, even on a bright sunshiny afternoon in spring, is a gloomy horror. It is a short street with grim old-built houses of darkened bricks and depressing alleys and courts. And the perfume! The new-comer, not warned in advance, will feel as if he had been smitten on the head or thumped in the stomach, or otherwise deadened and sickened by some sudden shock...stand for a few moments in the enclosed yard where the smell is well retained within the walls. As you breathe in the pungent odours you cough and spit, perhaps retch, for the acid vapours assail the lungs like poison and set up nausea. "It's only the vitriol, Sir," say the residents in these yards, "and sometimes the smell is better, sometimes worse. It's according how the wind blows."

Let's return to Love Lane and Buck Street for a peek at the interiors:

There is little furniture in their houses, but on the walls there is usually a portrait of a smart young soldier, given by his parents to the nation.

The walls are grim, desolate-looking, unpapered. The ceiling is low and, in some cases, thickly cobwebbed...Near the creaking door is the little fireplace, unguarded, of course, and a bit of cheap meat or a fish is being cooked in front of it. Two or three infants, half-naked, are sprawling about the bare floor.

Similar conditions were observed in St. Mary's ward:

...A woman sat sewing by the window. Two unwashed and nearly naked children were sprawling about the floor. Meat-bones, to which a cat was helping herself, were on the table. A man lay in the bed with bandaged head – he had been in a drunken brawl the night before and had split his skull. Rent of the room was four shillings.

In the second room was a soddened old woman. Amid the accumulated filth of a week or a month, the air pestiferous, the sole ornament a black bottle on the mantelpiece – rent of room four shillings.

In a third room were three tatterdemalion girls, doing nothing. They were going out at night. In addition to the bed was a wooden cot in which a fractious baby was screaming.

2. Essington Street. Forget the 'good old days', life for most was dour beyond description.

3. In 1890 Alice Cooper was discovered dying from starvation in her home in Grosvenor Street.

St Bartholomews was no more up-market:

> We went to a house where a woman, her husband and four children occupied a room. The children had not been properly dressed for the day or washed, and it would have been hard to say what their faces were like. The woman was dozing over a fire, her dress pinned at the neck, but otherwise open; the man, who was out of work, was snoring in a drunken sleep on a sofa with three legs, all shaky. One of the children was covered with sores; another had a diseased foot...The room stank with oppressive air, aided by the remains of two herrings lying on the wooden table and a bucket containing cabbage leaves and potato peelings in the corner. The window and the ceiling were cobwebbed. When we left the house the woman was dozing again already, and the sot on the sofa was still snoring.

Woman's lot was accepted by most as being one long round of child bearing and burying. Accommodation in the rapidly expanding city was so vastly overpriced large families, crowded into two or three rain-sodden rooms, were forced to take in lodgers. One twenty-year-old slept with the man she intended to marry together with his brother and the lodger in the same bed. She found nothing wrong with the arrangement as the lodger slept at her feet!

Most people managed to get enough food to exist, if not actually thrive. The typical diet of the poor consisted of white bread with bacon liquor or margarine and sloppy tea. Many of the 'lower classes' regarded vegetables as 'pig's meat'. Such was the precarious state of finances that whole families lived from hand to mouth. One reporter, observing the lives of the poor noted:

> Dinner that day had consisted of a copper's worth of fried fish. Where tomorrow's meal would come from could not be said.

Some, usually the elderly or very young, just faded away through lack of proper sustenance. In May 1890, Alice Cooper was found in her home in Grosvenor Street by her neighbour in a very weak state, slipping in and out of consciousness. Being a widow and unable to find work, she was forced to exist on just 7s. per week. With the rent amounting to some 4s. 6d., Alice and her four children were left with just 2s. 6d. for food and other expenses. Like the good mother she was, Alice put her children first. When eventually discovered by a neighbour Alice had not eaten for six days. Her body and clothes had not been washed for weeks. Propping her head up on her lap, the neighbour forced some brandy and milk down her throat and sent for the doctor.

A very weak pulse was found, warmth applied and suitable food sent for – all in vain. Alice died the following day with the cause of death listed as 'congestion of the lungs accelerated by want of food and attention.'

In the coroner's court a more blunt verdict of 'death from starvation' was recorded. A gift of £2 was handed to the family with the proviso that they should spend it on themselves and not their mother's funeral.

Serious cases of starvation and malnutrition continued well into the twentieth century. In February 1908 police burst into a home at 19, Back Inge Street. This was not a raid but a mission of mercy following reports by worried neighbours. The house was spotlessly clean but the officers were forced to recoil in horror at the sight of four emaciated people lying in the living room waiting for the grim reaper.

47-year-old Mrs. Emmanuel, her two daughters, Marion (20) and Rebecca (4) and her 17-year-old son could only have been a matter of days, perhaps hours from death.

Following the death of Mr. Emmanuel, the respectable Jewish family had fallen on hard times. Too proud to beg, the only job the mother could find was as a rag sorter, one of the dirtiest and worst paid jobs of the times. Mrs. Emmanuel, having been revived and nursed back to health, told police about the brutal facts of life among the poor and unemployed:

> I have had 14 children but 11 died. I had one son died when he was 21, a girl when she was 20, another girl at 15 and the last was a girl of 17 who died two years ago. We have had no work since Christmas and Christmas Day was the last we had a good meal. Since then it has been nothing but bread and tea except when the neighbours have bought in a little fish or meat.
>
> On Saturday there was nothing whatever to eat in the house. I got a cup of tea for the children and on Sunday morning we had another cup of tea from the same leaves. I shut the door for I felt ashamed and I felt I was a burden on the neighbours. Rather than be that I would die first.
>
> We do not want charity, we want work.

Living conditions in the slums were extremely harsh at the best of times. In the worst of times they were made almost impossible, particularly during a severe winter. Such was the case in February 1895, when temperatures lodged (four in a bed?) permanently below zero. Two intrepid, well-muffled reporters from the *Weekly Mercury* went to see how the poor were coping:

> We went into a house in Barn Street which is tenanted by a widow and her four children. They were huddled together for warmth on a wooden settle. No fire was in the grate but a candle was burning on the table, the little ones were trying one after the other to warm their perished hands. It was midday, and they had nothing to eat but a small loaf given them by a huckster who supplied them with the necessities of life.
>
> In the neighbourhood of Fazeley street nobody was working – even the rag and bone dealers could not sell their wares because nobody would come out of doors to inspect them. The wives of chimney sweeps, hawkers, musicians, painters, glaziers etc were forced to go to the pawn shop. The first goods to go were tables and chairs, then clothing and finally beds and bedding.

4. Mrs. Emmanuel was forced to sort rags, one of the poorest paid and dirtiest jobs. Following the death of 11 of her fourteen children, she locked herself in her home to await the grim reaper. This photo Coventry Street 1904.

5. Whole families lived in two or three rooms.

6. The rear of Rea Street

7. Garrison Lane, home of the mad axeman Thomas Clarke.

8. Back of no. 210, Francis Street.

Those who could not afford rent on a regular basis slept rough when out of funds and in common lodging houses – where no credit was ever given – when they had a few pennies. Many such establishments were to be found near Park Street. Let's take a brief glimpse at accommodation for the transient poor:

> *A dozen or more men, their ages varying from 18 to 80 [are] seated on wooden benches round a long and rickety table. The one cheerful feature in the room is the blazing fire on which a cauldron is seething and it might be a witches' cauldron judging by the whiffs of pungent odours which come from it.*
>
> *The air smells horribly of stale tobacco, cooking fish, cabbage-water, and bits of meat and bacon; the floor is filthy and sickening with mudstains and spittle; the walls are brown and sooty; the windows are thick with a fluffy accumulation of dust. But the inmates are one and all in a cheerful and reckless mood, smoking their pipes, eating out of the greasy parcels they draw from their pockets or their handkerchiefs, and telling each other ribald stories mixed with blasphemy and oaths which are regarded as the height of humour...*
>
> *Crime and cunning are stamped indelibly on most of the faces. At night they will go out for some hours to 'pick up' their living – or to be picked up.*
>
> *The women's 'common kitchen' is, if anything, viler than the men's. There is no air or cheerfulness about it; even the fire is duller, and the fact that some sloppy washing of rags is being perfunctorily performed adds to the general dreariness. Here again there are a dozen, perhaps twenty, people crowded.*
>
> *There are old women, with hair which would be white were it cleaner, their faces weary, their eyes dim, their lips tremulous. They crouch with folded hands silently near the fire, and they appear to be in the last stages of exhaustion.*
>
> *There are women of middle-age with hard faces and knotted hands, defiant of mien, bitter of tongue, strong, but with the despair of life's failure printed as plainly as in letters upon their sullen faces.*
>
> *There are young women, untidy, unashamed, with loud voices and ready laughter, with wicked looks and leers, with a fearful mockery upon their lips in various stages of disgrace and ruin which can only end in the depths others have reached.*

9. Ada Watson, 35-year-old habitual drinker put on the black list in 1904.

10. Margaret Rooney, 39 in 1872. Hair: grey. Eyes: grey. Life: grey. One of many Irish immigrants to Birmingham, Margaret's sad accusing eyes seem to follow you everywhere. A truly haunting photograph evoking the spirit of the age when life for many was brutal beyond description. For the record Margaret's sole conviction was for petty larceny. 7 days hard labour to add to her 39 years.

The nightlife on the streets was something else:

> Boys and girls go shouting along. Drunken men are arm-in-arm with drunken trollops, singing pantomime songs in maudlin voices. Gangs of youths are playing football in the streets. A youth goes by with a concertina, fingering out with hideous discords the captivating air of 'Little Milly, She Was So Silly' while a dozen raucous voices join in the exasperating chorus of 'La, la la.!' Three girls, hatless, almost shoeless, their ragged dresses pinned up at the back, follow them, eager to attract attention by shrieking with that shrill forced laughter…
>
> A huge-limbed man of not more than 25, with close-cropped hair, big ears and a bull-dog mouth, starts a quarrel with a diminutive girl, who cannot be more than 18, carrying a pallid-faced six-month baby in her arms. The girl appears to plead with him and he listens with a cruel tightening of the lips, and suddenly his clenched hand flashes out. She is down, baby and all. He gives a contemptuous glance at the prostrate figure and the screaming child and shambles into the corner public-house where he is lost to sight. The girl rises slowly, bleeding at the lip, convulsed with sobs, picks up her infant, stares round vaguely, and then realising the hopelessness of all things, slowly limps away.

Such was a typical Birmingham street scene, though one that might have been played out in any large industrial city one hundred years ago. The incident was observed before a reporter of the *Birmingham Daily Gazette* in 1901. Life, for most people in the capital of the West Midlands, was harsh, brutish and rife with violence. The only pleasure, for some, was a pint or ten at the local. Moreover, drunkenness was a temporary escape from the hopelessness of many Brummies' lives. One of the most popular pub crawls was from Deritend to the Bull Ring, drinking a half pint in each pub.

Drunkenness was far from being a problem confined to the male sex, as a report from 1870 confirms:

> …The drunken women squatted themselves on the pavement, and howling and laughing by turns, invited the officer to 'come on' while the boys delighted with this determined attitude, cheered for the 'ladies' and then called on the 'Bobby' to 'go in and win.' …
>
> Presently five policemen were seen approaching at a quick pace pushing a curious kind of brown wickerwork carriage, mounted on four strong low wheels – a sort of giant perambulator so constructed that its occupant might recline at full length. The laughter with which this cumbrous vehicle was received was hearty and general. The police advanced into the yard, and soon reappeared with the corporation perambulator occupied by one of the lady bacchantes… one plump-faced matron was seen stretched at full length, winking, smiling, nodding and kissing her hand to her helmeted escort.

DISGRACEFUL SCENE IN THE STREETS OF BIRMINGHAM.—UPROARIOUS CONDUCT OF DRUNKEN WOMEN.

11. 1870 - drunken women rounded up for transporting to the police station. The transport resembled a giant wickerwork perambulator. The ladies illustrated here were described as 'respectable women who met in a public-house off Bull-street every Tuesday morning.'

dents depicted the city as a new Sodom and Gomorrah, whilst police and council reports described a relative Garden of Eden. The truth, like the prostitutes, probably lay somewhere in between. An annual inspection of brothels – for statistical purposes – was part of the policeman's job. They were instructed to list the number of girls under sixteen and total the number of bawdy houses. 1876 *official* Birmingham figures list 175 brothels housing a grand total of 213 pavement princesses, with numbers decreasing towards the end of the century.

Officially counted or otherwise, brothels hid a multitude of sins. In 1870 P.C. Green testified that it was not safe for an officer to be alone in a brothel in Great Brook Street. He had intervened in a dispute where the only discharge a punter effected was in the shape of a stone through the window!

Agreeing with P.C. Green, P.C. Hobson displayed particular hostility towards three houses in the Brook Street Yard, occupied by fifteen women. Pulling no punches, he told the court that in his opinion, these particular establishments should be burnt to the ground. On looking through the details of his colleagues' misdemeanours, however, it's clear they did not share his apprehensions.

12. Catherine Durkin, an habitual drinker, could never go to the police station without a fight. Her only periods of sobriety were those under lock and key.

For men a short encounter with one of the streetwalkers was another flight from reality. A graphic description of night life at the turn of the century lists the common meeting points between John and Jill.

> Even early in the evening no decent person can walk without trepidation down Livery Street, down Digbeth and Deritend, along Cheapside, and all the purlieus, without needing to be well on his guard. Impudent solicitation by women of all ages, and the more dangerous molestation of the men who chiefly live on these women's earnings, are a common experience. I spent a Saturday in these neighbourhoods recently, and carried away the ineradicable impression that they were wholly given up to drink, violence, and debauchery. Men and women rolled about the streets in intoxication, quarrelled with each other, and menaced peaceful pedestrians, and the air was filled with the foulness of oaths and blasphemy.
>
> As night came on crowds continually gathered at the corners of the streets to witness a fight, to listen to a woman's ravings, or to watch the ejectment of unruly characters from ale-houses.

Figures for the number of *erring sisters* in Birmingham in the 1800s are very unreliable. Religious correspon-

13. Even the most mild-mannered of men resorted to violence if they felt cheated in brothels. Punters were often fleeced before, after or even during coitus, which was often interrupted by a 'bully' who sent the customer packing, his tail between his legs.
Though not in the way he originally intended, Joseph Lestor was eventually discharged. Is he trying to communicate with the police photographer?

14. Nellie Jones alias Brown and Painter. Numerous convictions for soliciting and prostitution in Handsworth 1904-05. Usually fined five or ten shillings.

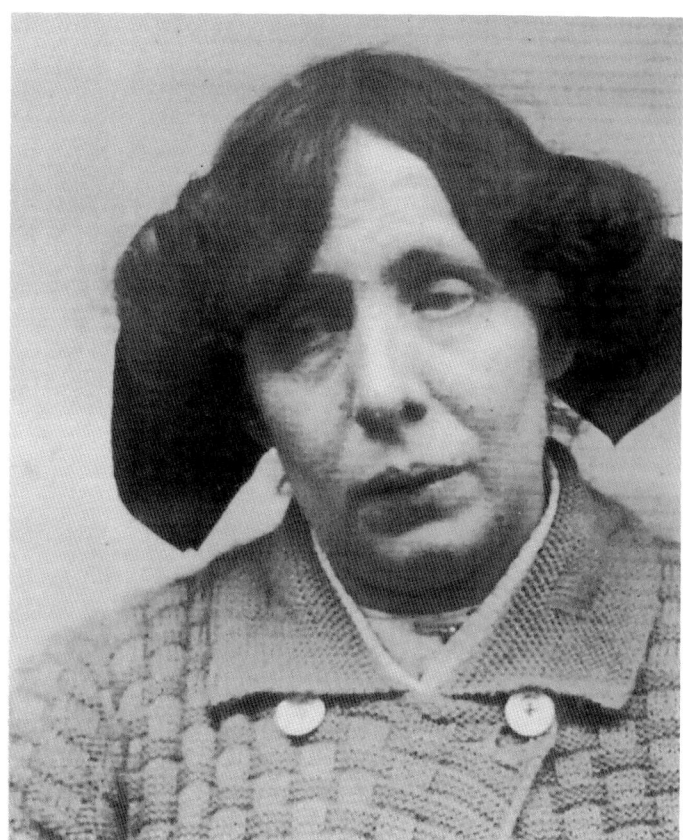

15. 29-year-old Gertrude Myers received two punishments for soliciting in 1913. After her two weeks inside she was deported back to Germany.

Every large city has its sexual side, though this report from Brum's Victorian times is probably just a little exaggerated:

> Every wall, every corner, every entry every doorway even is put to infamous use. The wall round the church in this slum has had to be raised because the buttresses of the sacred edifice were used every night by couples, and some of the women had frequented the place so long and regularly that they had been able to set up a right to a particular portion...A respectable woman who resides in a front house was disturbed by a noise at her door. She opened it and a man and a woman fell in.
>
> A girl of fourteen secured admission by craft a few nights ago to an outhouse in a yard some distance from her home. Suspicion was aroused as to her conduct, and in a few minutes an investigation was made. A man was found with her, and two others were waiting. The girl's mother was informed of the facts. She was indignant – at the complaint! 'What does it matter to anybody,' she demanded 'if a girl can't bring a few coppers home?'

We assume she was talking cash.

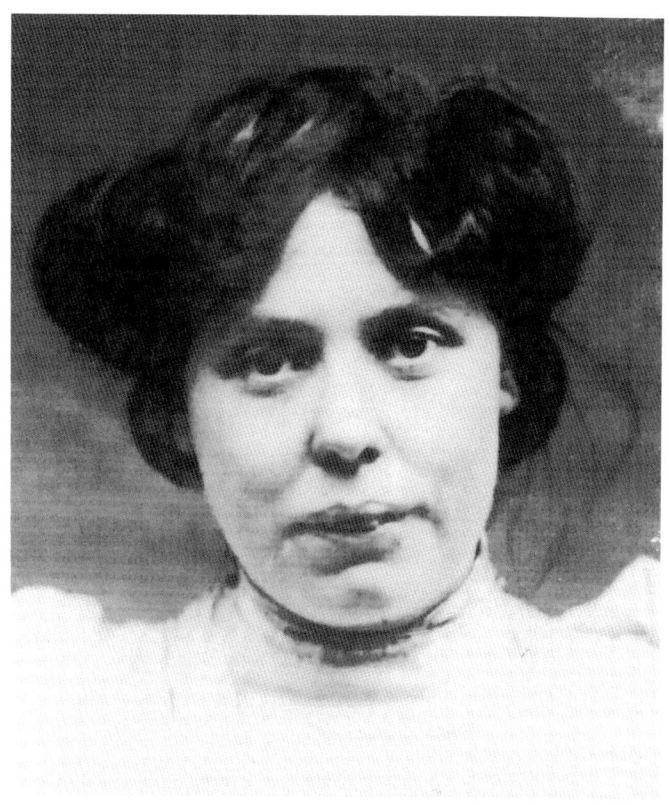

16. It appears there was one law for locals and another for foreigners. In 1911 Annie Davies was charged with keeping a brothel. She was fined £5 and ordered to pay costs. That same year Emma Goldman wrote about the problems faced by the Gertrudes and Annies of Birmingham. 'Whether our reformers admit it or not the economic and social inferiority of women is responsible for prostitution.'

Not all mothers were this indifferent as to the fate of their daughters. One woman was clearly distraught upon hearing about her offspring's latest position:

> 'My little girl' she wailed 'as I tried to take so much care of! – gone away with that vile wretch who keeps a _____ house. I've lost her. I shall never see her again. Her father says it'll kill him. The woman came to live near us, noticed her, took a fancy to her and has led her off.'

Girls would approach men in the street and invite them to their rooms or down dark alleyways, though the boys' assets were more likely to be 'snatched' in the sense they had not intended! And some women wouldn't take no for an answer. On October 22nd 1869, Emma Edwards of 6, Spring Hill and Charlotte Evans of New Canal Street were charged with soliciting. They followed a man to the Oratory and asked him to go home with them. Not wanting to be the meat in the sandwich our hero declined but the girls were so insistent he gave them 6d. each to leave him alone and then complained to the police. The women were each fined a very hefty 40s. or one month imprisonment.

While many prostitutes had their bullies or pimps, their married counterparts had husbands, who were often no better.

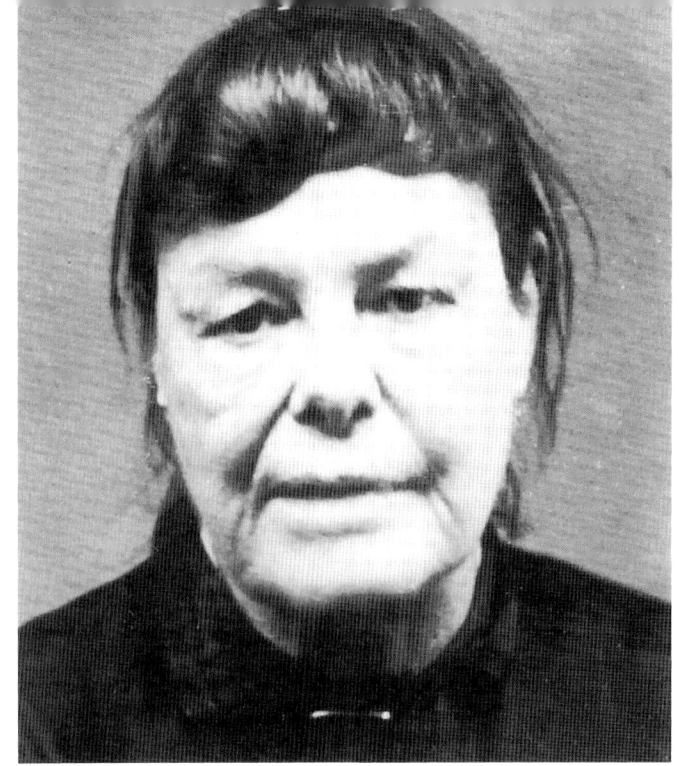

17. Some women, no longer able to work as prostitutes, took desperate gambles to earn a little drinking money. In 1909 Jane Jarvis was charged with housebreaking. She was 68 years old! The gallivanting Granny was found 'not guilty' and discharged.

18. 4-7 Great Brook Street. In 1870 a P.C. Green told the court it was dangerous for policemen to enter a brothel here alone. They probably came in pairs.

'A WOMAN, A DOG AND A WALNUT TREE'

19. Wives would be assaulted for 'offences' such as not providing mackerel for supper.

Commenting in 1902 on one of the many cases of wife-beating that came before the courts in Birmingham a judge observed:

> The old saying 'a woman, a dog and a walnut tree; the more you beat them the better they be' has its believers amongst the lower classes.

Two years after passing his 'walnut tree' remark the same judge, displaying an astonishing degree of prescience, passed lengthy sentence on an offending husband with the observation:

> As I have said before you men seem to make footballs of your wives. I have no patience with you.

The popular penchant for domestic brutality was highlighted by the media of the day. In a newspaper article 'Slumland' dated 1901 a reporter noted:

> Next to constable baiting comes the less exciting, but very satisfying pastime of wife-beating but the prosecution of the brutes who engage in it is seldom understood...A woman gave birth to twins. The same night her husband dragged her and the infants into the street and left them there in the drenching rain, in order that he and another woman could occupy the room.

In the 1800s beating one's wife was almost the norm for brutish Brummies of low self-esteem, who invariably blamed their partners for the sheer drudgery and harshness of their lives. Whether in or out of work, many husbands sought relief from the confines of their lives at the local hostelry. As far as the men were concerned wives were little more than warders, moaning and nagging incessantly for money to buy such luxuries as food. They deserved a good kicking and they usually got it.

Penalties for the widespread pastime of wife-beating were no deterrent to the brutal bullies who took out their self-loathing in this way. Women lived in constant terror of husbands' *playful habit* of keeping swords and razors under their pillows. Often women did not bring cases against their men, fearing the retaliation of being thrown destitute onto the street.

DRUNKEN FOOL OR DRUNKEN FALL?

In 1894 Thomas Grayless *a rough looking fellow* was charged with violently assaulting his paramour. He was given into custody for kicking out five of Catherine Baggott's teeth. The now dentally challenged victim testified in court that the injuries were caused by a drunken fall, not a drunken fool.

The following incredulous version of events was put before the magistrates. After telling the court that she fell against the table Catherine Baggott (C.B.) was questioned by Mr King, the magistrate's clerk (M.C.)

M.C: *What did you give him into custody for?*
C.B: *I told the policeman he had kicked me, but he didn't.*
M.C: *Was your mouth bleeding?*
C.B: *A little.*
M.C: *What about your teeth. Did you see the policeman find any of them on the floor?*
C.B: *Yes, two of them were loose and I pulled them out for aggravation.*
M.C: *How many did you lose?*
C.B: *Four.*
M.C: *How were they loosened?*
C.B: *With the force I suppose of knocking against the table. I was very drunk.*
M.C: *Do you say he didn't strike any blow at all?*
C.B: *No, Sir.*
M.C: *You gave him in charge and told the policeman he kicked you?*
C.B: *Yes, I was excited.*
M.C: *Has he ever struck you before?*
C.B: *No, Sir.*
M.C: *Have you ever brought him before the magistrates?*
C.B: *Yes, once I had a bit of a row with him.*

Normally the reluctance of a witness to prosecute would have led to the charge being dismissed. In this case, however, police caught Grayless literally red-handed, his fist covered in the blood of his partner, the defendant was sent down for two months.

'A TWO HOURS FIGHT WITH A WIFE':

Some matrimonial disputes became marathon affairs. In July 1896 Edward Robinson, 34, of Francis Street was charged with having assaulted his wife. Both parties appeared in court with their heads bandaged. Mrs Robinson, who did not really want to press charges, gave evidence with great reluctance. She stated that her husband came home and threw *an American meat can* at her.

Mr. King: (Magistrate's clerk) *What did it do?*
Mrs. Robinson: *It missed me.*
Mr. King: *Well how did you get injured?*
Mrs. Robinson: *We were both on the floor and fighting together. I gave him a crack, and he hit me with something.*

Police Constable West stated that when he visited the house he found the pair scrapping on the floor. He was a good community copper and stayed a full hour to calm both sides down. No sooner had he turned his back, however, than the pair tore into each other again. Mrs. Robinson chose as her weapon a kettle of hot water, while her husband favoured the American cans. To cries of "here's to you" Mrs Robinson hurled scolding water from one side of the room while corned beef flew from the other.

The bench thought the pair had been punished enough and adjourned the case…until the next time.

20. *Francis Street 1905, scene of the civil war between the Robinsons. His favourite weapons were tins of corned beef, Mrs. Robinson retaliated with scalding water.*

21. Coventry Street 1904. Women were sent to fetch jugs of beer and often incurred the wrath of their husband if they took too long about it

22. Sheep Street where all many women got for Christmas was a black eye!

A BOY AND GIRL MARRIAGE.

Some couples didn't even have the memory of a honeymoon period. Again in 1896 a young man, described as 'an undersized youth dressed in the attire of the peaky' (a reference to the infamous Peaky Blinders) appeared in court on a *neglecting to maintain* charge brought by his wife. The magistrate thought that the couple looked little more than children and asked their ages. The girl replied they were both nineteen and had been married six weeks. It hadn't taken her husband long to show the bullying side to his nature. On their wedding day he threw an oven-plate at his bride for refusing to fetch beer on tick. The magistrate, Mr. Lancaster, showed an unusual interest in the case:

> Lancaster: *Where did you go for the honeymoon?*
> Complainant: *We didn't have one.*
> Lancaster: *It was a kicking moon I should think.*

The young bride said that she did not want her husband to go to prison so the case was adjourned.

Michael Ryan's wife also dropped allegations of assault following a beating in April 1872 but once again police evidence was enough to send the hectoring husband down for two months. When sentenced Ryan seemed to treat his enforced absence as something of a break:

> Well, that's a good job. I shall be rid of my beautiful wife for a time.

The feeling was certainly mutual.

LIKE A WILD BEAST

1897 saw a more serious case. A man beat his wife to death because, by a process of convoluted thinking, he blamed her for the loss of two fingers. A few months earlier he'd punched her in the mouth, cutting his fist on her teeth. Perhaps predictably, the two fingers had become so infected they were eventually amputated.

The behaviour of one bruiser only came to light in the course of another case. In January 1870 Thomas Walters, a butcher in more ways than one, was summoned for drunkenness and the use of foul language. One Saturday night he was seen leaving his Drake's Cross home and was, as usual, well bowsered. He unleashed a torrent of foul language at his sister in the street and was immediately arrested.

It came out in court that Walters' wife was confined to bed with a broken thigh, the result of an earlier accident caused by Walter's drunken driving. Having been thrown from a horse and trap, the unfortunate Mrs Walters had been ordered onto her feet by her husband, who'd stood over her, whip in hand, threatening to kill her if she didn't get up.

Walters, when sober, was a well-conducted man, but stewed as a prune, he was *perfectly mad, more like a wild beast* and habitually ill-treated his wife. He had, in fact, been before the magistrates several times. On this occasion, a surgeon stated that Mrs Walters would never recover unless removed from her husband's violence and drunkenness. Walters was sentenced to seven days with no option of a fine, not long enough for his battered wife, who seemed destined for the most wretched of lives.

Some ten years later 43-year-old Henry Cheston of Frinton Street was charged with assaulting his wife, Ann, with kitchen equipment. Returning from the boozer, he hammered Ann to the floor and hurled all the household silverware and cups and saucers at the distraught woman. He followed these with the spittoon before dragging her and their two children to the door and giving them the key to the streets. Even when the hapless Ann Cheston returned with a policeman, her husband was not intimidated and got in one last kick to her stomach before being arrested. In this case the wife did press charges and her husband had two months to sober up in Winson Green.

CHRISTMAS CRACKERS

In 1884 a report was presented to the Artizans Dwellings Committee describing home life in some of the worst areas of the city. Lench Street, Potter Street, Price Street, Sheep Street and Cliveland Street were singled out as having the most impoverished inhabitants housed in the most overcrowded slums. Many houses were mini battle zones:

> *I found a very large number of women with black eyes a few days after Christmas, many of whom seemed to regard a black eye as part of their Christmas festivities. Many of those whom I found in bed had been drunk overnight.*
>
> *In some streets – Sheep Street for example – one woman in every four or five seemed to have a black eye. As to the poverty and misfortune, I found a woman making 'tack boxes' at 2d. a gross, or turning and remaking trousers at from 5d. to 7d. a pair and, thus, I suppose sometimes spreading contagious diseases.*

A FEW BOILED POTATOES

We all know how serious arguments often arise from the most trivial of perceived offences, the squeezing of the toothpaste in the middle of the tube rather than from the bottom for example (I'm a middle man myself). Often overreaction to such minor indiscretions led to a serious bout of fisticuffs. Most rows concerned proffered food.

In 1873 Edward Sands set about his wife Catherine in their home in Newton Street. Sands admitted the assault but told the court he was provoked because his wife was always drunk and could not be bothered with his meals.

On the day of the attack he had walked many miles and put in a hard day's work only to be rewarded with a Spartan supper of a few boiled potatoes. Magistrate Jaffrey characterised the assault as brutal, cowardly and murderous, adding that but for the mitigating circumstances (Mrs Sands' dipsomania) he would have inflicted a heavier punishment than the three months hard labour he duly handed down.

In 1895 a man referred to in the press as a 'brutal husband and father' ferociously struck his wife about the head with a coal hammer because she could not produce mackerel for his supper. All she could rustle up at 1am was a plate of liver and bacon.

The drunkard insisted he was not going to have any of that _____ stuff, though obviously changed his mind the next morning, getting stuck into a nice piece of 'back'. Unfortunately it was his wife's back he bit before turning his self-loathing onto his two-year-old child. For the next twelve months he could only dream about liver and bacon.

23. Cliveland Street, one of the most deprived and overcrowded slum areas of the city.

24. In 1873 Edward Sands set about his wife in their Newton Street home. She had served but a few boiled spuds for his supper. It was three months hard labour with better meals to follow.

MAD WITH PASSION

When well-oiled, husbands and wives would often threaten 'to do' for each other and the result of drunken brawls was occasionally more permanent than the odd cut, bruise or broken bone. The civil war in the Appleby household had been going on for some time. In 1878 John Appleby's home in Emily Street was the scene of many a late night set-to between this professional wife-beater and his beaten wife, a drama usually played out in front of their daughter.

In early February 1878 Appleby seized a carving knife and threatened to slit his wife's throat. A week later, in his usual drunkard state and mouthing obscenities, the toolmaker arrived home and, according to the daughter, was 'mad with passion'. His wife tried to escape his attentions by rushing out of the house but seizing her around the neck, he pulled her inside and violently slammed the door. The daughter escaped into the streets, screaming for help to anyone in the neighbourhood: *Good God, he has killed my mother.*

Mrs. Appleby was found dead at the bottom of the cellar steps. Her husband, showing little concern, stated she had fallen accidentally, a tale apparently bought by the judge.

THE TINGLES TANGLE

October 16th, 1880 saw Mr Tingle in the local bar preparing himself to deliver his wife's weekly thrashing. At home, meanwhile, Mrs. Tingle prepared herself to receive it. She hated her husband's foul temper, it being excessively swift when liberally soused. She waited, apprehensive but determined, to confront the slobbering, smelly swine now unrecognisable from the swain she'd wed. The Tingles had tangled before, with Mrs T. waking, on a good day, with black eyes and bruised ribs.

This time, Mr. Tingle tumbled into the living room redolent of the stink of distilled humanity. Back in his own private prison, he knew that a torrent of abuse was about to begin. A few seconds after the door slammed the neighbours were tuning in to the foul language and savage insults the couple had been mentally preparing throughout the evening.

Soon fists were flying. Caught by a heavy blow, Mrs. Tingle instinctively reached for something with which to defend herself. The nearest object was the paraffin lamp, which Mrs Tingle unhesitatingly smashed over her husband's head. Alerted by the smoke, neighbours forced the door. They were confronted by a drunken

25. A typical product of Summer Lane, John Baker (a future football fan?) was found guilty in 1874 of maliciously wounding his wife Susan. He got twelve months hard labour.

26. Yet another row and Mrs. Tingle attacks her drunken husband with the paraffin lamp. Both died from burns a few days later.

abuser writhing in agony in a chair, his hair and clothes ablaze, blood streaming from a deep gash in his forehead.

Barely clinging to life Tingle was rushed to Birmingham General Hospital where he died a most painful death a few hours later. Most of his last words were incoherent or obscene, but pointing to his wife he was heard to moan: *She did it.*

Mrs. Tingle was also hospitalised for serious burns, doctors and nurses guessing she had sustained her fatal injuries by attempting to smother the flames that engulfed her husband. The neighbours, however, knew better. The Tingles were inseparable, death was no escape. Aptly prepared for his ultimate destination by the means of his departure, were Tingle and his wife united down below?

The leniency of sentencing in serious cases of wife-beating, attempted murder and manslaughter might be considered disgraceful by today's standards. In rare cases it was possible for individuals travelling on the train without a valid ticket to spend more time in prison than men who made their women's lives a misery. A brief resume of cases in the 1880s and 1890s almost beggars belief.

In 1889 a 38-year-old baker from Lozells Street was charged with attempting to murder his wife by shooting her with a revolver. The charge was reduced to 'shooting with intent to do bodily harm'. He was sent down for six months.

In a similar case that same year the licensed victualler of the White Hart Inn in Cromwell Street discharged a loaded shotgun at his wife following a domestic dispute. Fortunately the woman was only grazed. Another lenient sentence of five months was given.

In 1894 34-year-old Henry Hadley of Hope Street, motivated by jealousy, was convicted of attempting to murder his wife by cutting her throat with a razor. He was bound over to keep the peace!

Those whose actions resulted in the deaths of their nearest and dearest were no more harshly punished. In 1899 John Crowson told a neighbour 'I and my wife have had a few words and she has dropped down dead.' The doctor found a bruise on the left cheek and a cut on the right ear. The defence argued that death may have resulted from a fall against an open door and the jury agreed there was no case to answer.

In 1893 Walter Coldrick's wife jumped through a window in Tennant Street whilst fleeing from her drunken assailant. She died from her injuries. He was sent down for eighteen months.

William Drenman caused the death of his lover, Mary Phillips, by striking her on the head with a teapot. He received the comparatively strong sentence of three years. On March 8th 1891 Henry Spears, an electrician from Rea Street, killed Catherine Gallagher by throwing a paraffin lamp over her and setting her alight. At the coroner's court a verdict of wilful murder was returned, but again this was reduced to manslaughter at trial and a sentence of eighteen months passed.

27. Harry Holcroft shot his wife in Great Russell Street in 1891. He was sentenced to nine months for manslaughter.

28. Despite having teeth knocked out, ribs broken and bodies bruised, wives were reluctant to testify against brutish husbands.

Harry Holcroft, alias Cook, an eighteen-year-old ironcaster from Great Russell Street, was also found responsible, by the coroner's court, of the wilful murder of Maud Mansell. Having shot Miss Mansell with a revolver on 31st. January 1891, Holcroft was tried at Birmingham Assizes and walked from prison a free and fitter man nine months later.

I LOVE MY DOG

Following an N.S.P.C.C. investigation in 1907 Robert Milner of house 7, 33 court, Heage Street stood in the dock for neglecting his wife and children. Milner loved his dog more than his family and was probably barking mad. Throughout his trial Milner regularly interrupted proceedings. Reflecting his pet interests, he would come out with such remarks as *'I'll have a monkey next'*.

Whilst his wife and three children, the eldest of whom was 15, slept in one bedroom, the second bedroom was set aside for the dog, with Milner insisting that the mutt have a feathered bed, whilst the children make do with dirty sacking.

The canine lover's wife was forced to prepare the best meat for the pet; sausage and bacon went to her husband. It was vegetables for herself and their three children and all on two shillings a week. Milner justified this meagre contribution to the family budget by blaming his wife's profligacy:

She's tipsy three or four times a week and I'll never have a tipsy woman round me. The public-house is too near and the things go too fast. This shirt (he partly took off his coat) has been on for three weeks. There's no monkey as tricky as a woman.

After having previously been sentenced to three month's imprisonment for having assaulted his wife, a separation order was made on this occasion with Milner directed to pay eight shillings weekly.

LIVING IN SIN

Given the acrimonious quarrels and physical violence so common between husband and wife, it is surprising that couples married at all. But that they should do so a second time, and that whilst currently wed, certainly shows the triumph of hope over experience! Whilst serious cases of wife-beating and assault merited terms of imprisonment measured in months, the punishment for bigamy or trigamy sometimes resulted in the offender serving a year per partner.

Thirty-year-old Edwin Charles Morris, a theatrical performer, practiced his profession both on and off the stage. Morris was brought before the court at the instigation of his second wife, the grandly named Josephine Fredericia de Escofet. He was charged with having bigamously married Josephine in Birmingham on 29th September 1867 whilst his former wife, the more prosaic Sarah Moss, was still alive. The first wedding had taken place in Liverpool in 1858.

Edwin and his second 'wife' had spent a tempestuous three years together. They wed because Josephine wanted the local priest off her back. He was forever berating her for living in sin. Josephine knew Morris was married when she walked down the aisle with him. He had made no secret of the fact. But due to his violent disposition Josephine had told him 'not tonight' and left him on at least fourteen occasions before finally shopping him for bigamy. Edwin, who was blind, defended himself in a voluble cross-examination and Josephine finally admitted she had conspired in the bigamy. Objecting to the harsh line of questioning from her partner she commented:

I did not know you were a Lawyer.

To loud laughter from the court the actor retorted:

I have been in gaol four months and that is enough to make any man a lawyer.

29. The infamous 'Peakies' at home in Clyde Street.

30. William Drenman smashed a teapot over his lover's head in Rea Street. Another murder charged reduced to manslaughter - 18 months.

He then turned to the judge and, making a polite bow, added:

I beg your pardon my Lord.

Edwin was now centre stage. Determined to display his skills to gain sympathy from the court, he gave a brief resume of his life story. As a lad he had been a sailor. Returning to the port of Liverpool in 1858, he had met and married Sarah Morris. Because there was no work in Liverpool, however, almost at once he returned to his mother in Birmingham. Sarah refused to accompany him. Over the next few years the enterprising Edwin earned his livelihood in theatres and concert halls. He probably had his fingers crossed when he told the Judge he'd had news of his first wife's death.

Chastised for beating his wife, the beak then sentenced him harshly on the charge of bigamy. Edwin burst into tears upon receiving his two year sentence, repeating over and over:

Do bear me one word, my Lord.

He was led from the dock crying and wringing his hands in the most piteous manner. It was his last performance for some time.

That same year, Thomas Poulton, who deserted his wife and nine children to bigamously remarry, was sentenced to a mere twelve months. The fate of his abandoned children is unrecorded.

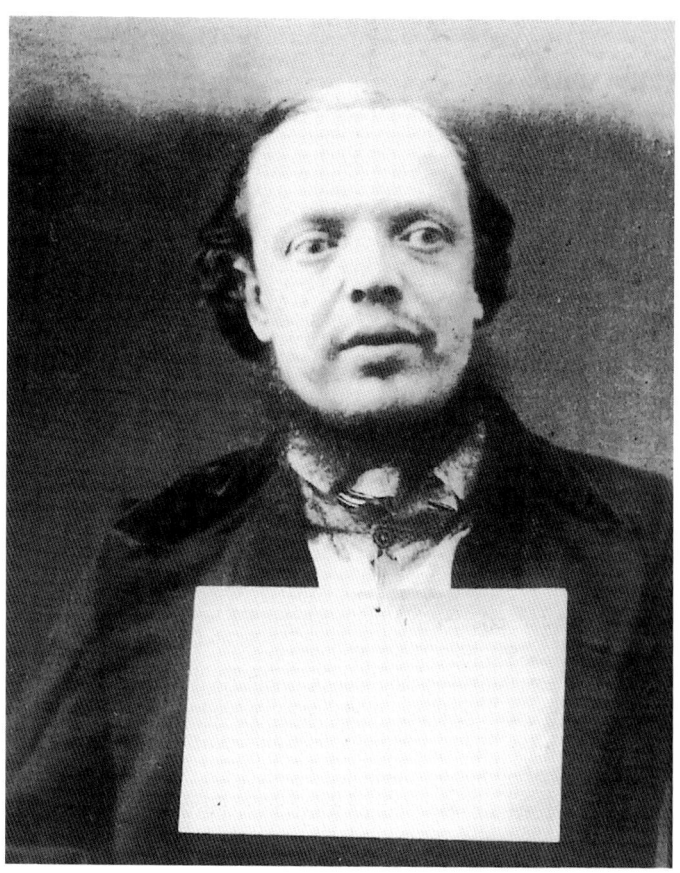

31. Blind actor Edward Morris was sentenced to two years for bigamy. This was a particularly harsh punishment when compared with the typical three months for wife-beating. The 32-year-old was led from the dock crying and wringing his hands in the most piteous manner. No Oscars followed.

32. Wife-beating was the norm in many households.

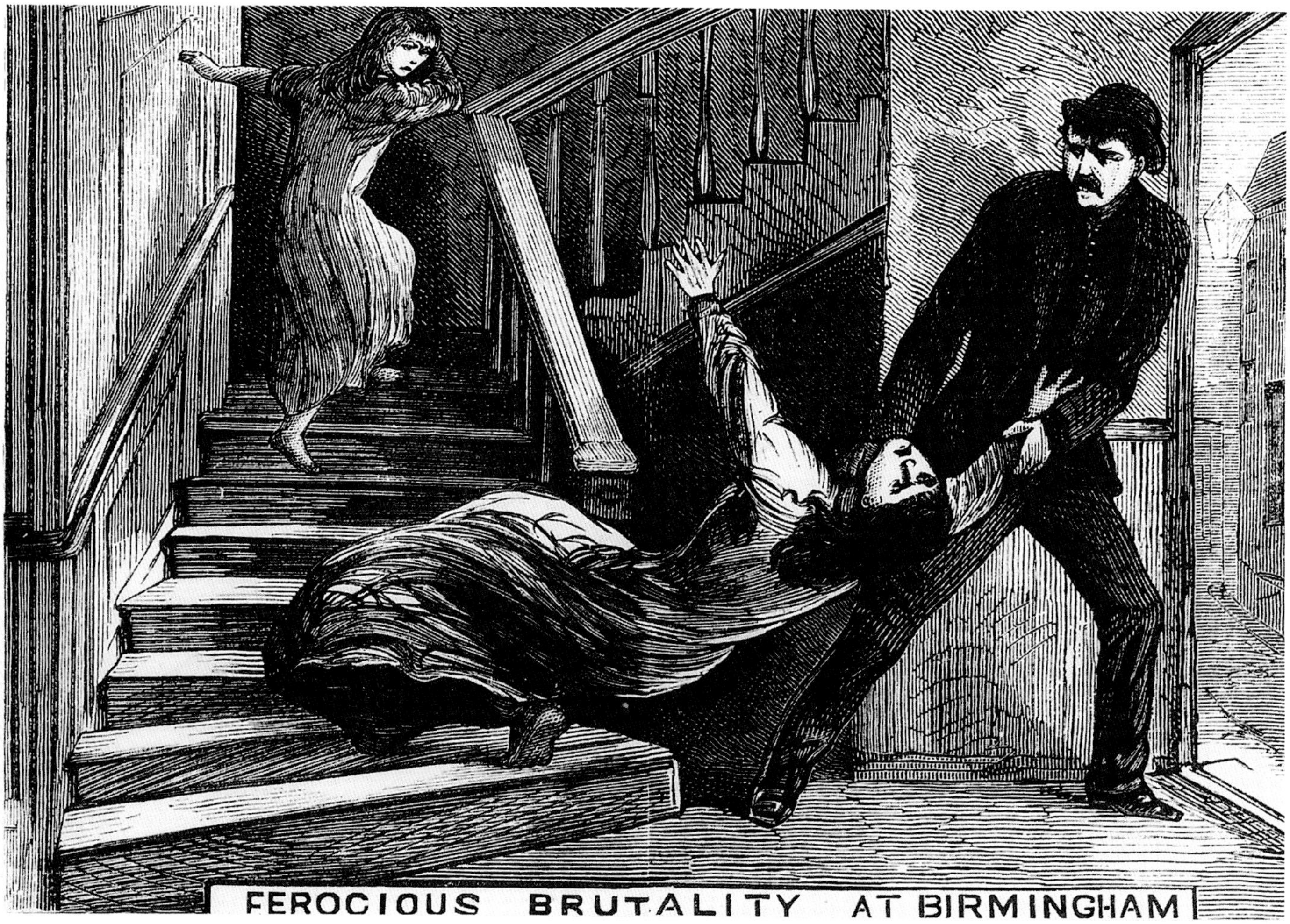

THE VISITATION OF GOD

Buried four, only this one left.
Buried six, been married twelve years.

Such were the commonplace replies to questions posed to mothers about their children, in Birmingham's poorest parts. Most deaths were imputed to natural causes or *the visitation of God*. Some cases, however, were extremely suspicious. Children placed an enormous burden on the family budget and when women *fell*, due to the absence of effective methods of birth control, many opted to take a gamble with the backstreet abortionist.

Rebecca Simister could not face the rigours of childbirth a seventh time. Contacting the midwife, who had helped deliver five of her six children, Rebecca pleaded with 57-year-old Sarah Ann Eden to help terminate the pregnancy. The year was 1895. An extremely crude operation was performed, probably with the ubiquitous knitting needle, and six days later Rebecca, wife of Thomas and mother to six youngsters, was lying on a slab.

At the post-mortem doctors found 'certain wounds' and came to the conclusion that they were inflicted by a single thrust of a sharp instrument. The cause of death was blood poisoning.

Before her premature demise Rebecca told her husband about the 'operation'. An incensed Thomas tackled the midwife shortly after his wife's death. Sarah Eden pleaded for his silence:

Oh Mr. Simister. You won't tell the doctors what your wife told you will you?
What I did I did for her good, Mr. Simister. I never used any instruments on her. I never used them. I would not have done anything to hurt her. I loved her so well.

The pleas fell on deaf ears. Throughout her trial for murder Sarah Eden insisted she had been wronged and when found guilty feebly repeated; *I am innocent. I am innocent. I am innocent.* Sentenced to death she fainted into the arms of the warders and had to be carried from the dock. Although a capital sentence was occasionally passed in such cases, it was rarely enforced. Sarah Eden never met the hangman.

The poorer classes were forced to rely on women who knew about such matters as abortion. The wealthier classes consulted doctors more than willing to engage in a little lucrative overtime. The extra payments did not always guarantee quality of service, however. In March 1912 Lena Kinmend and her maid took the short train ride from Coventry to Birmingham. At New Street the couple met up with Alice Cake, who acted as a go-between for customers wanting abortions and doctors willing to undertake the job. The three women went to a doctor's surgery in Sherlock Street where elementary surgery was completed in less than three minutes.

A short time later Lena fell seriously ill with peritonitis, caused by a septic instrument which had bought about a partial abortion. The job had been seriously botched. Before she died Lena made a statement to the police incriminating both Dr. Arthur Austin and Alice Cake. She had paid the former £8 and the latter £2. When informed of the death of Mrs. Kinmend, all Alice could think to say was:

Oh God in heaven. I didn't even have a cup of tea with her.

The jury were out for fifty minutes and the lesser verdict of manslaughter was returned. Austin was sent down for seven years while Cake was canned for six months being a mere accessory.

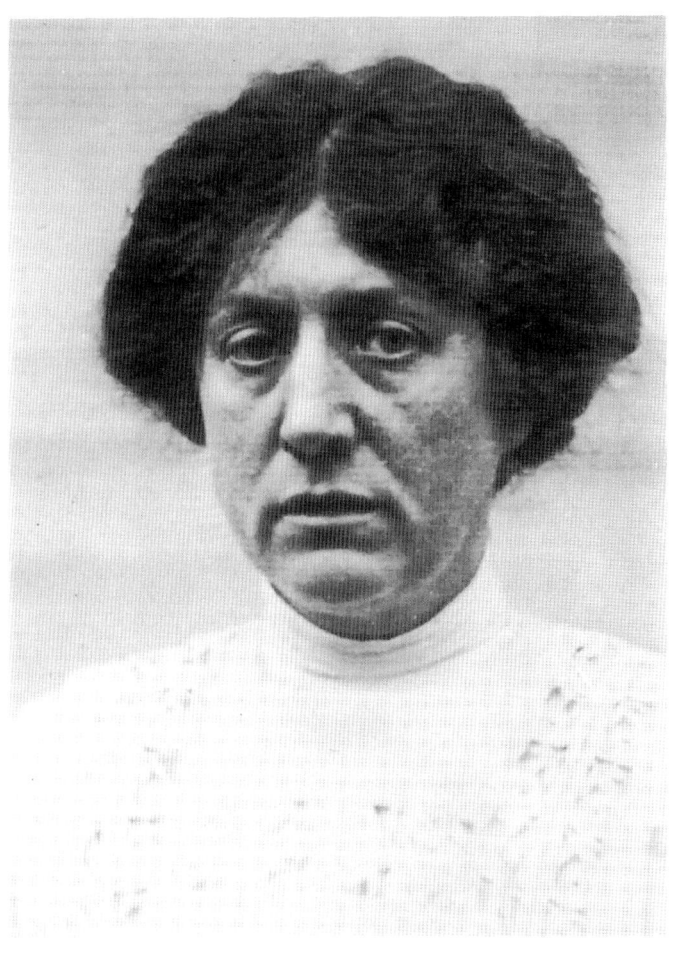

33. When told of the death of a woman whose abortion she had arranged, all Alice Cake could say was 'I didn't even have a cup of tea with her.'

Quite how very young babies met their death was always difficult to prove. In July 1880, 53-year-old George Pope Garlick was trading as a chemist and druggist at 40, Vauxhall Road. When police raided his shop they discovered the remains of three new born infants. In court Detective Ashby testified that an inquest had been held on one of the bodies and a verdict of 'still-born' returned. The other bodies were deemed too young to have inquests held upon them. In the absence of evidence against him the prisoner was ordered to be released. We'll never know if Garlick had any guilty secrets, though the following is quite suggestive:

PRISONER: *What I am done with?*
SUPERINTENDENT HALL: (dock-keeper) *You are discharged. Won't that suit you?*
PRISONER: (smiling) *I should think it will.*

In the same year a young woman living in Parker's Building, Highgate Street went to answer a call of nature. In the pan of the closet attached to the house lay a smallish foul-smelling 'bundle'. The police constable called to the scene would later describe 'the body of a male child, in an advanced state of decomposition, wrapped up in some linen and a piece of black rag'. The pathetic remains were taken to Moseley Street where it was found impossible to say whether the boy, whose remains were now one month old, had been born dead or whether he had met a violent death. The jury returned a verdict of 'found dead' and the matter was swiftly forgotten.

Eight years later a charge of murder against 20-year-old Fanny Mitchell was reduced to 'concealment of birth'. She disposed of her unwanted baby by stuffing a piece of rag in its mouth and concealing the body in an ashpit in Tower Street. Fanny was sent down for eighteen months. Life was very cheap.

The discovery of dead and abandoned babies did not cause the controversy it does today. In Victorian Birmingham, such finds were almost to be expected as an order, passed to P.C.s in 1858, indicates:

> *All children found dead by police constables to be conveyed to the nearest station which is in the parish that the body was found in.*

Even more than thirty years later baby's bodies appeared more an inconvenience than the subject of full investigations. In the chief constable's report from 1891 he appears resigned to the fact that such cases would never be solved:

> *The body of a full-grown infant (female) was found in Holliday Passage on 20th. August, 1891 by two youths, named Joseph Coppage of Farm Street and George Garrett, Latimer Street South. The coroner's jury returned a verdict of wilful murder against some person or persons unknown. Notwithstanding the police have made a rigorous investigation into the facts of the case, no one has up to the present been arrested.*

Although no laughing matter, the scene played out in court in the trial of Harriet Jervis in 1872 held a certain degree of black humour.

The evidence against the 19-year-old servant was so strong that few denied her guilt. Harriet's employers accused her of being pregnant but she insisted she was just a normal healthy girl, still growing. When the body of a newly born baby was discovered under a heap of stones in the closet the finger of suspicion immediately fell on the servant who was duly charged with 'concealment of birth'.

After consulting for a few minutes the jury returned a verdict of 'not guilty'. The decision caused such astonishment in court that one of the juryman felt obliged to inform the judge that eleven voted for a verdict of 'guilty', but the foreman thought otherwise and had given in his personal verdict to the court. (Laughter).

The judge reprimanded the foreman and instructed the jury to consult again. The decision had to be unanimous otherwise there could be no verdict. The foreman apologised saying that this was his first appearance on a jury and that he had understood they all believed the prisoner to be 'not guilty'. When a second verdict of 'guilty' was returned the judge enquired whether this was the opinion of all present. He was answered by a dumb silence. The foreman was sulking, and, after an embarrassing few seconds, the fourth juryman in the box rose and agreed the case was proved. A new foreman was elected and Harriet was sent down for two months.

A nurse who worked with the poor was not surprised at the high number of premature deaths. In an article published in 1907 she pulled no punches:

> *Mothers murder their children. It is nothing less than murder. They give the little babies gin, brandy and whisky which makes them almost insensible, and of course, sends them to sleep. There are scores of babies who meet a premature death simply through drink, and doctors have told me that upon examination infants have been found to have died from drunkards' liver. I believe the cause is heredity...*
>
> *I don't think there is a city in England where there are so many women ignorant of household duties as in Birmingham. We give them lessons upon the care of children, but they are callous and indifferent and have no wish to be interested in the matter.*

The nurse had some sympathy with young baby-minders. Some as young as six years old were expected to look after younger siblings:

> *A little girl is not the proper person to be in charge. And who can blame her if a baby is found to be bruised about the body when it is having it's daily bath. I said 'daily bath'. Ah how much more healthy the little babies would be if they were washed daily. I have seen some that had not been washed for a week and their mothers had not a suitable utensil in which to hold the water.*
>
> *I was in one house last week where an old meat tin was used for washing the household clothes, cooking and washing the baby.*

One case enshrouded in mystery never reached the courts in 1887 due to a lack of evidence. Ten-year-old Alice Forrester and her twelve-year-old brother were arrested on suspicion of having caused the death of a baby, Minnie Fereday, by slashing her legs and feet at No. 2 Clifton Place, Asylum Road.

Clare Wilkins from St Andrews Road couldn't even be bothered to name her fourth child. Born on the last day of 1901, the baby saw just twenty days of the new year before being squashed by its mother in bed.

34. Mason's orphanage 1908. No way to start a life.

35. Then, as now, children from broken homes were far more likely to deviate into a life of crime.

As a lawyer for the N.S.P.C.C. outlined the facts of the tragedy in court, the callous twenty-year-old mother paid little attention. Having married at fifteen, Clare had mothered four children by the age of twenty, three of whom had died. The midwife testified that, when born, the latest baby had been plump, not that the mother would have noticed as she was 'beastly drunk' throughout the birth and had a reserve supply of two pots of beer standing by with which to wet the baby's head.

When examined after death and twenty days of his mother's care, the infant, whose life had been insured, was in a filthy state and little more than skin and bone. Asked if she had anything to say Clare, showing little concern for her dead child, replied: *I hardly had any beer*. When the defendant promised to take the pledge sentence was deferred for one month to see if she could keep her word.

Some mothers could not discard their children to the elements. In February 1874 Eliza Watts, a servant, gave birth to twins. The girl was healthy but the boy very sickly. Along with her porter husband, 21-year-old Charles, she was indicted for having unlawfully abandoned a male child under 2, endangering the life of the child. This case, however, was not as clear cut as it first appeared. The couple had taken the sickly boy to a prosperous property on the outskirts of town where, after wrapping him in a thick coat, they gently placed him on the lawn, believing that the people who lived there would take care of their son. They left a false note with the child implying that the boy had been born out of wedlock and abandoned for these reasons. It read:

Henry Belcher, born 25th February 1874 in Gooch Street. Oh blame me not, but blame rather the man that has deceived me.

The couple hid behind bushes until they saw that their baby had been discovered and taken indoors. There is no information as to how the pair were tracked down but they were probably shopped by neighbours or the midwife. Both were found not guilty of intending to destroy human life, and, as they had been in remand for over two months, were sentenced to a further six weeks on a lesser charge.

For slum children who survived birth and the ravishes of disease, deprivation and a poor diet, life was extremely harsh, both at home and on the streets. Children were sometimes used as pawns between rowing parents.

30-year-old Jane Freer, her baby nestling for warmth snugly at her bosom, was doggedly trailing her husband along the towing path by the canal near the Golden Hillock Road. They had had another domestic and he was abandoning both mother and child. The absconder suddenly turned sharply on his heels to confront his wife. His message was curt: *If you come a step further I will*

36. *Both trains and stations have long been associated with crime. Thieves, pickpockets, prostitutes and perverts mingled with travellers. Children risked death by wandering onto the tracks and many juvenile offenders started lives of crime by throwing stones at trains.*

37. Bad lads or bad dads? John Kelly, 15. 4' 6" 3 months for stealing champagne. John Smith, 12. 4' 1". 21 days, 5 years reformatory for a similar offence. Charles Lambourne, 10. 4' 1" 7 days and a whipping. Stealing frock from father.

throw you and child into the water. Jane, now almost out of her mind, had nothing to lose. She replied: *I won't give you the chance.*

Kneeling down at the edge of the towing path, she lowered her baby into the canal. Luckily for everyone concerned in the 1886 drama some passers-by intervened and rescued the baby from a watery grave. Whether either parent would have let the child drown will never precisely be known, but the stipendiary magistrate did not believe Jane had really intended to take her baby's life and the case against her was dismissed.

On the rare occasions that parents could afford new clothes they inadvertently put their children at risk of attack from *child strippers* like 17-year-old Eliza Hunter of Harding Street.

Using sweetmeats as bait she would entice children into water closets and strip them of their clothing. One Saturday morning in 1872 Ellen Hyde from St. Marks Street frantically began scouring the roads and alleyways in her neighbourhood. Her daughter had been missing for over two hours. Spotting a large crowd in Summer Hill she was both shocked and somewhat relieved to see her daughter clasped tightly in the arms of another woman. Her daughter's boots and flannel petticoat were nowhere to be seen. The woman was Eliza Hunter who would later face two charges of stripping, having removed all the clothing of another young girl, whom she'd abandoned, naked and shivering, in a W.C. That petrified trembling waif had been taken back to her home by a constable.

In court two pawnbrokers gave evidence that Eliza tried to pledge clothes. Sentencing her to six months with hard labour the judge admonished the teenager for being *'a very cruel, artful and wicked girl'*.

Far greater danger lay in the home than the streets. Many children were regularly given a hefty clip round the ear for transgressing family rules – usually made and enforced off the cuff – by drunken dads. Some sadistic parents went further. For severely thrashing his 5-year-old daughter with a horsewhip in 1897, Edwin Bull was fined forty shillings. The bully of Browning Street sought to justify his actions by telling the court that his daughter had stolen some money and he was determined to give her *'a thrashing she would not soon forget.'*

Other children were simply in the wrong place when their parents lost their tempers. In 1894 Walter Newcombe threw a large jug at his wife, but with his aim unsure the missile fatally struck his fourteen-year-old daughter. He served six months for manslaughter. That same year Robert Collins was struck on the head with a poker in New Summer Street. The ten-year-old died from his injuries. His mother was sent to prison for two months.

A report in the *Birmingham Weekly Illustrated Mercury* in September 1907 laments the lack of leisure and play time in many children's lives:

There can be no doubt that in Birmingham a vast amount of cruelty is inflicted upon children of tender years whose misfortune is to belong to poverty-stricken parents, to be denied the opportunity of play and childish recreation owing to be forced to assist at every available moment at hook and eye carding, paper box making and baby minding etc…There are not hundreds but thousands of poor children living in this city in a state of semi-starvation.

The same year a *Tribune* reporter visited Birmingham. His description of conditions was not over-flattering:

In the next house I visit there are six children. The children are without clothing and in a vile condition and there are no signs of any food being provided. There is no coal in the place and the grate shows that no fire had been lighted for some considerable time.

When a doctor called, the reporter continued, he visibly reeled back with a cry of terror when he saw a living skeleton. The child on the bed, which should have weighed about 48lbs. was no more than 15lbs. Another child, found lying on the stairs had its mouth and nostrils so furred with filth that it could scarcely breathe. The widowed mother had spent every penny of the husband's insurance money on drink.

Seven years earlier another medical man stumbled across a similar scene in 26, Kitchener Street. Dr. Trout had been called in by the N.S.P.C.C. to inspect the home of Stephen and Mary Jane Carr. The stench made the doctor gag as he set about his grisly probings. The bodies of the four children aged from six months to twelve years were covered with vermin marks and dirt. They were forced to sleep on a bed 'which no ordinary language could describe.' Both parents were dipsomaniacs. Stephen got 30 days, Mary 90 and the doctor four hundred fleas!

In August 1904 Walter and Mary Boswell were sent down for one month each for neglecting their four children. In the youngster's bedroom – which the parents never entered – maggots up to a half inch long were discovered sharing the filthy blankets.

Boys and girls under ten were expected to contribute as best they could to the family budget. One 9-year-old boy's typical day saw him rising at 6am from a bed in which his father, mother and three brothers and sisters also slept. He took breakfast at the board school and after lessons was taken to various taverns to entertain the drunkards with his singing. His earnings for the fifteen hour day were not even enough to afford decent clothing, his attire being described by a reporter as a man's coat whose cut-down tails touched the ground. 'His shirt was black and in rents; hat, vest, boots and stockings he had none'.

If anything life was more difficult for girls. One ten-year-old lived in a two-bedroomed house with fourteen persons, members of her family and lodgers.

She regularly puts in her five-and-a-half hours at school, and is a well-conducted and intelligent child. For two-and-a-half hours every night she looks after a neighbour's baby, and on Saturday is engaged on that drudgery from 2.p.m. until 9.p.m. She earns 4d. a week.

Callous though it may appear today, some boys in their early teens were deliberately 'shopped' by their parents. Adolescent appetites made a big hole in the family budget. Accordingly, both true and trumped-up accusations of sons stealing their fathers' clothes were made to the police. Invariably the courts praised parents for their honesty, while sentencing the young vagabonds and urchins to five years in a reformatory. In this way the state assumed responsibility for youngsters' board and lodging. Thus parents acquired a little more ale money while their sons got three meals a day. It comes as no surprise, that after being shopped or framed by their own parents, many such youths declared war on society, becoming lifelong offenders.

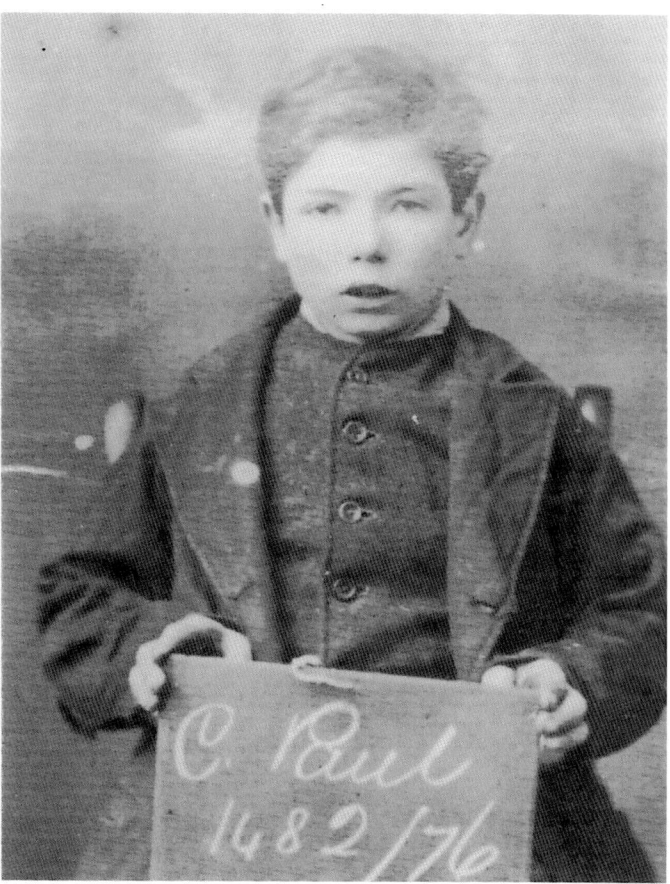

38. *13-year-old Charles Paul allegedly stole six pairs of his father's drawers. Charles got 14 days in an adult gaol, followed by five years in a reformatory.*

Eight-year-old Frederick Hemming, the son of a brass founder from Back 44 Constitution Hill was charged with stealing two shillings from his mother. Instead of the groceries on his list the young lad returned with a new hat – value one shilling, and a 4d. coconut. The balance had been spent riding on the steam train to Aston. Affirming to the court that she wished to prosecute, Mrs Hemming added: *I can't do anything with him. He won't go to school and always spends the money.*

Frederick was sent to the workhouse for one week.

Life on the outside was occasionally far harder than any prison regime. In 1886 a young lad was sentenced to solitary confinement and virtual starvation by his father. Charles Tipping, a 35-year-old cellarman, had taken to the bottle, or more appropriately in his case, to the barrel. His permanent inebriation had driven out his wife one year previously while he automatically retained custody of their two sons. One used to help him at work, the other was an inconvenience. The younger boy, who was not named in court, was left locked up in the family home in Lea Bank Square. But for the attentions of the neighbours, who encouraged him to exit via the kitchen window and fed him scraps, he may well have starved to death.

39. The younger Tipping was left to starve whilst his father worked and drank. Sympathetic neighbours use a clothes pole to pass up food to the child.

When the father found out about his son's forays from the house he barricaded the bedroom which led to the kitchen and threatened neighbours with the police if they interfered. The only recourse for the weakened waif was to stand pitifully at the upstairs window crying for food. One of the neighbours, a Mrs. Buzzard, took pity on the lad and, over the next fortnight, passed him food attached to the end of her clothes pole.

The police were eventually informed of the situation. P.C. Downing forced entry into the kitchen were he found the cupboard bare and no trace of fire in the grate. Breaking into the bedroom the officer discovered the naked little lad. Neither boy nor bedding had been washed for weeks and the young Tipping was in a very poor state, suffering from starvation and bronchitis. At Ladywood Police Station the liberated lad tucked into the standard police fare 'with avidity'.

On returning home in his usual drunken state, the wicked father went straight to gaol to report his missing son. The wind was taken out of his sails when he was informed that his son was in the back room taking a nap, his stomach full for the first time in months.

Charles Tipping denied neglecting the child so forcefully that he was locked up for being drunk and disorderly, for which he was later fined 2s. 6d. The magistrates ordered police to make further inquiries into the case of the neglected boy.

In 1888 Charles Hudson of Richard Street was prosecuted for allowing his 9-year-old daughter to sell matches after 9 pm. Elizabeth was discovered alone, plying her trade at 10.30 pm. The labourer, who was fined five shillings, was genuinely perplexed by the case. How could he be responsible for his daughter when he was asleep in bed?!

Some six years later a widower, Samuel Poole, a hawker from King Street and Elizabeth Higginson, whom he employed to look after his daughters, stood in the dock accused of neglecting the children, Alice Beatrice (11) and Violet Maud (9). The girls, half-naked and unwashed, were regularly sent out late at night to sell firewood. An N.S.P.C.C. inspector who visited their lodgings found Alice dressed in dirty rags swarming with vermin, though Violet was a little cleaner. Their bed consisted of a quantity of flock thrown onto the floor, topped with a few old coats for blankets. If the Society had not dressed them, the girls could not have appeared in court.

Both girls testified that they were forced onto the streets until 11pm in order to sell firewood. If caught in a downpour they were obliged to sleep in their wet wear. The clothes given to them at school were pawned by their minder in order to buy beer. These tailored garments were replaced by ragged lengths of old cloth, wrapped around their thin bodies and fastened with pins. Their undergarments were similarly fashioned. When they needed to find their father the girls would wander from one public house to another until they stumbled across the negligent oaf. The father was sentenced to two months inside and the minder one.

The girls probably ended up in the workhouse but may have been taken into a home and later 'exported' to Canada. That same year, 1894, a report was published by the Children's Emigration Homes. This organisation had been founded in 1872 for the purpose of rescuing boys and girls likely to follow lives of crime or pauperism. Between 1872-94, 2,139 boys and girls from Birmingham were shipped abroad to a 'better' life.

Once overseas, younger children were adopted and adolescents received wages of between twenty and sixty dollars per annum. The organisation proudly boasted that no suitable case was ever turned away.

Although one can see merits in the system, it was not properly thought through. Children were often separated from their brothers and sisters forever. Some were exploited and/or sexually abused with no-one to turn to for help. Lost, lonely and loveless the human surplus of Birmingham were destined to lead their lives thousands of miles from their blood relations.

The exploitation of children wasn't confined to the colonies, nor were matches their only merchandise. In a report on *juvenile depravity* in Birmingham, entitled *The Sin of Our Cities*, a special correspondent set out to expose the horrors of life on the streets:

> Some months ago I was standing at the foot of the steps in Station Street, waiting for a tramcar. I was pestered by a little girl, who, with the usual whine, said, Please buy a box of matches, sir; buy the last box. When she had repeated it once or twice I replied, 'No; go away. I've got some matches'; whereupon she made an indecent proposal.

> On Saturday month another girl, about twelve years of age, beset me with similar petitions on one of the platforms in New Street Station, and when I said I wanted no matches she looked about cautiously, and, dropping her voice, asked whether she should come into the carriage in which I was sitting.

The author went on to specify the service provided by match and flower sellers in the vicinity of the station. Still insufficiently outraged he sought fresh pastures.

> A few nights ago, wishing to ascertain facts, if possible, I made a journey down Deritend, a district with a bad reputation, and lounged about the streets which are in the neighbourhood of a cheap concert-hall. Hereabout can always be found a number of girls vending cheap articles, and towards midnight their importunity is very marked. A girl with tousled hair, decidedly young, stunted in growth and with something of a withered look upon a face that might have looked fresh and winsome, accosted me, and, as it was not my purpose to discourage her, speedily revealed her horrible profession. She had a few boxes of matches in her pocket and she offered them for sale; but for a little higher remuneration she was willing – nay, eager to "take me home." "Who lives with you?" I asked. "Uncle and his missis" was the reply, the last word leaving me in no doubt as to whether the "missis" was in the eye of the law the girl's aunt. "Will they let me come with you?" I inquired. "Oh, they won't care" said the girl, "especially if you was to get 'em a drink".

Let's rejoin the author on a bitingly cold January evening:

> I was walking down Martineau Street, one of the large, new thoroughfares of which Birmingham boasts. Four girls, bareheaded with gaudy shawls thrown over their shoulders, the eldest of them looking not more than fourteen and the youngest of them, though with a wan, haggard face which told its own tale of misery, seeming to be about ten, were just in front of me. One of them came up with an impudent leer and in a coarse voice exclaimed "Mister give me a penny," and being refused, passed on and rejoined her companions, who had turned off abruptly and were waiting round a corner. Presently I heard the following conversation between the girls:
> "Sarah how much do you charge the fellows now?" "Anything they like" came the ready reply; a penny, or I'd even take a ha'penny."

Forced to share rooms with one or both parents regularly inebriated there was little privacy for children in the majority of Victorian households. Youngsters witnessed at first hand the so called facts of life at a very early age. A reporter at the turn of the century described this early loss of innocence:

> ...boys and girls alike become familiar from infancy with every detail of sexual relationship in the squalid

and overcrowded homes where husband and wife, brothers and sisters, old and young, herd together like rabbits in a warren. There is no modesty, no reserve, no delicacy in our slums, and the passions of children are prematurely developed, while eye and ear are fed with disgusting sights and words which make morality, and not its opposite, a mystery.

Children were malnourished and prone to disease, forced to sleep with their siblings, and sometimes their parents too, under cover of the night and old clothes. Many girls were forced to endure the unwanted sexual advances of elder brothers or fathers. The reporter who wrote our introduction to Birmingham night life at the turn of the century hinted at a crime that would not be openly admitted and discussed for many decades to come:

And, most ghastly of all, the overcrowding favours bestiality in general, and the relations between fathers and daughters, uncles and nieces, mothers and their own sons, is such as we dare not describe.

Incest was also hinted at in a report for the Modern Review:

The Inspector of the Society for the Prevention of Cruelty to Children says: "I know that the conditions under which many children are raised in Birmingham must tend to corrupt them and deprive them of any sense of morality, or decency, or modesty. The one-room and two-room tenements are most common; they may be found in street after street in numerous localities. The condition of life for children in these tenements is shocking, and I hear of terrible cases of unnatural outrage and vice. The cases are very difficult to prove, yet I know they exist."

We can only guess at the frequency of incest in Victorian Birmingham. Both victims and perpetrators normally chose the path of silence. Just one case from the small number that reached the courts in 1870 helps to illustrate the problem and the punishment deemed appropriate at the time.

In February of that year George Pretty was charged with committing a rape upon his own daughter. Mary Ann Pretty was sixteen at the time of the offence and her father 44.

George left the house for work one day but returned a few minutes later. When asked by his daughter why he replied: *I have to be at a warehouse in Bradford Street by eleven o'clock and I am going to sit here until I go.*

Her father then suddenly seized Mary and half-carrying and half-pushing forced her upstairs where he raped her. This was not the first time he had had his wicked way with his own daughter but on this occasion her mother found her in such a distressed state that she soon guessed at the truth and reported the matter to the police. When questioned in court, the rapist, putting his handkerchief to his face and speaking in a whining voice, said he was very sorry it had happened. He was duly sentenced to six months with hard labour.

Sometimes family members could not live with the consequences of their own actions following the discovery of an improper relationship. In January 1895, Caroline Birch, 18 and her stepfather Edwin Birch, 35, were discovered in a field lying side by side. The girl's throat had been cut and both had swallowed more than enough carbolic acid to have caused death.

40. 23-year-old William Smith was sentenced to twelve calendar months for the rape of a young girl, Ann Walker. The brassfounder from Gosta Green insisted the girl had consented but the judge admonished him, saying that consent was no plea.

With such poor guidance exhibited by parents the antisocial behaviour of even very young children was almost to be expected. This was combatted, with little effect, with the stick, when the carrot may well have been more appropriate.

BORN TO BE WILD

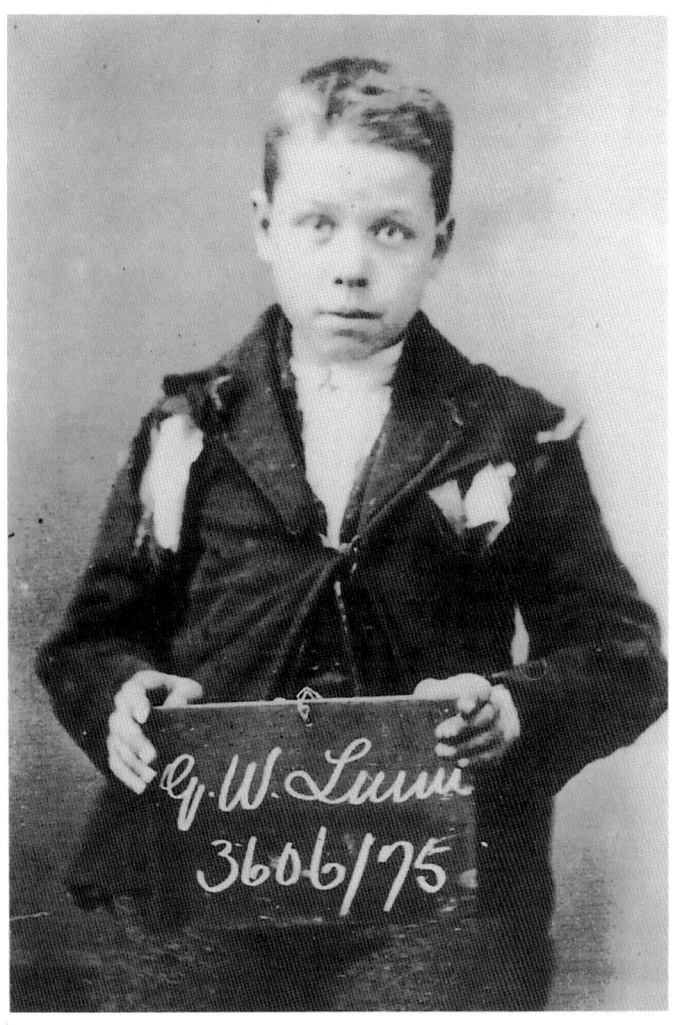

41. George Lunn. The 14-year-old was sentenced to five years in a reformatory for petty theft. Charges were sometimes trumped up by parents to get shot of their youngsters.

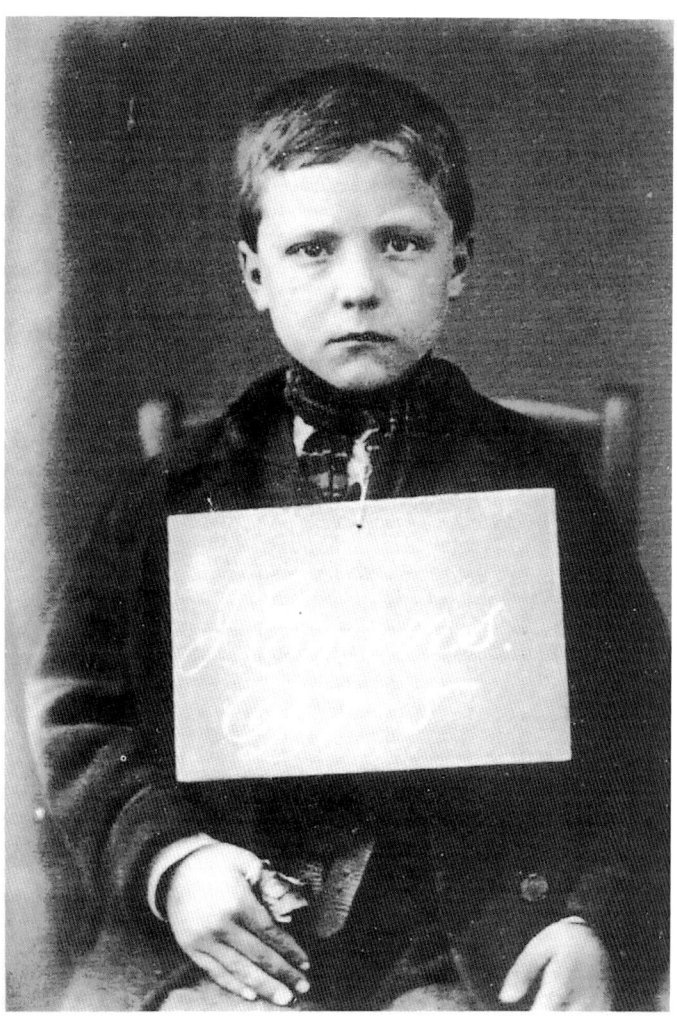

42. James Evans (11) was whipped and sentenced to one day's imprisonment for stealing two books. The short, sharp shock didn't work. He was back in court again four months later facing a charge of simple larceny. Six weeks hard labour were followed by five years at reform school.

Looking through the mug shots of Winson Green prisoners in the 1870s, one can't help noticing the high number of fresh-faced boys, many under five feet tall and garbed in rags, who were sentenced to a whipping, a short term in prison and a long term in a designated reformatory. The most common offences committed by pre-pubescent boys involved petty larceny, gambling, stone throwing, obstruction, cruelty to animals, sleeping out, begging, housebreaking and wilful damage.

Some hardy souls even attempted to assault the police, who doubtless doled out summary punishment before the culprit even saw the magistrate.

James Evans was described in a newspaper as being an 'old young thief'. He tried to better himself by stealing two books in February 1872, but didn't learn his lesson of a good whipping. A few months later he stood, all 4' 2" of him, before the court on a second charge. This time, the ten-year-old was arraigned for stealing a pocket handkerchief from his employer in Silversmith Street.

James told his mother he found the fashion accessory but knowing her son's ways Mrs Evans determined to follow the path of hard love and put him on the straight and narrow. She didn't pawn the handkerchief as most would have done, but returned it to its rightful owner. As a result, young James was convicted of simple larceny in the summer of 1872. He was sentenced to six weeks' hard labour followed by five years in a reformatory.

James was probably given hard labour 'of the second class' – shoemaking, tailoring, mat making, oakum-picking, brush-making, carpentry or upholstery and would have followed a regime similar to that of the Gem Street Industrial School given on page 40:

43. Edward Timms from Loveday Street. Another boy sent to pass his adolescence in reform school for petty larceny. Photos from the early 1870s offer a good insight into contemporary street chic.

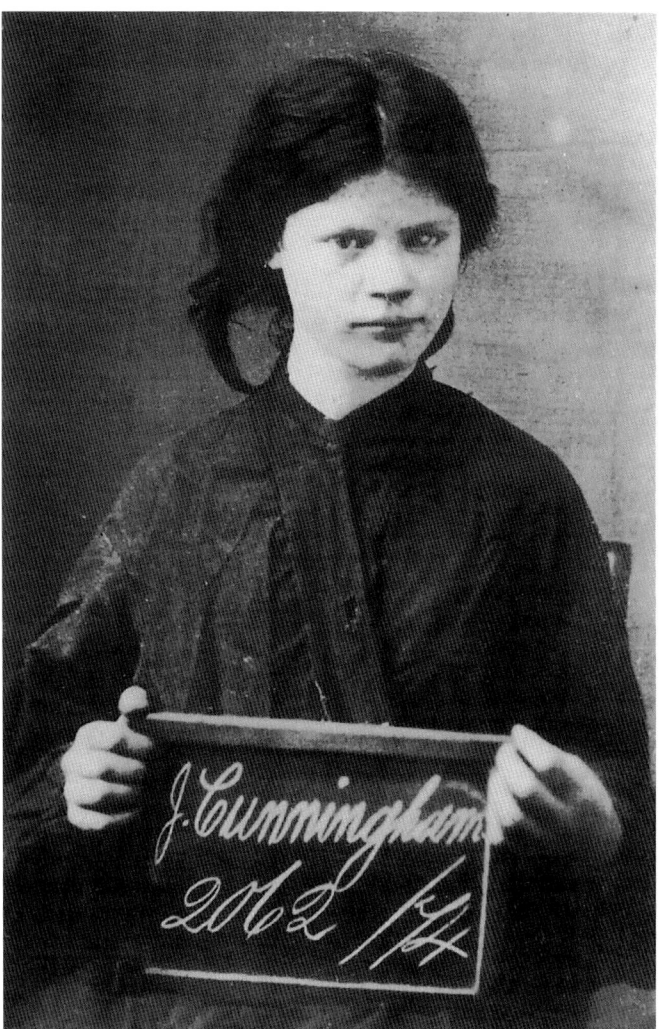

44-45. 14-year-old Julia Cunningham was found guilty of stealing a pair of boots. The sentence, '3 + 3 calendar months' seems harsh for a first offence.

Girls had a slightly different regime. Instead of recreation and exercise their time was spent on 'domestic duties' while afternoons were sweated out in sewing classes.

Industrial School meals look monotonous and almost certainly included food and drink of the lowest quality, but many outsiders envied the guaranteed regularity with which they appeared.

Bread appeared at sixteen of the twenty-one meals and spam not once – no great surprise since it hadn't been invented!

Some observers thought the schools were, dare we say it, the best thing since sliced bread, which also hadn't been invented, whilst others pointed out that many of the young male graduates went on to a life of crime. A school supporter, however, noted:

6.00 – 7.30.	Rise, clean shoes and dormitories and wash
7.30 – 8.30.	Prayers and breakfast
8.30 – 9.00.	Recreation
9.00 – 12.00.	School
12.00 – 12.30.	Exercise
12.30 – 1.00.	Dinner
1.00 – 1.30.	Recreation
1.30 – 5.45.	Workshops
6.00 – 6.30.	Tea
6.30 – 8.00.	School, prayers and retire

	BREAKFAST	DINNER	SUPPER
S.	Bread, butter, coffee	Roast meat, vegetables	Tea, bread and butter
M.	Coffee, bread	Bread and cheese	Milk and bread
T.	Bread and milk	Roast meat, vegetables	Bread, dripping, coffee
W.	Bread and coffee	Fruit and suet pudding	Bread and milk
T	Bread and milk	Roast meat, vegetables	Bread, dripping, coffee
F.	Bread and coffee	Liver, vegetables	Bread and milk
S.	Bread and milk	Coffee and bread	Bread, treacle, coffee

46. 15-year-old clog-maker Henry Wilson stood just 4' 3" in his stockinged feet. Another 'volunteer' for reform school.

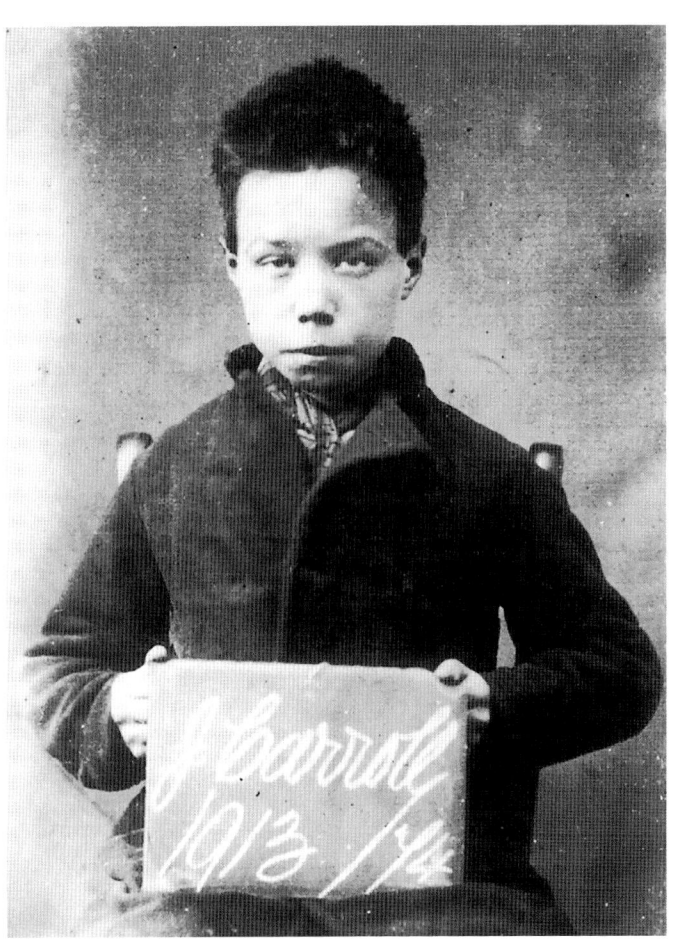

47. 12-year-old James Carroll served six weeks hard labour for being a 'rogue and vagabond' - surely a misprint 'lovable rogue' would be more appropriate. He was another destined for five years in the reformatory.

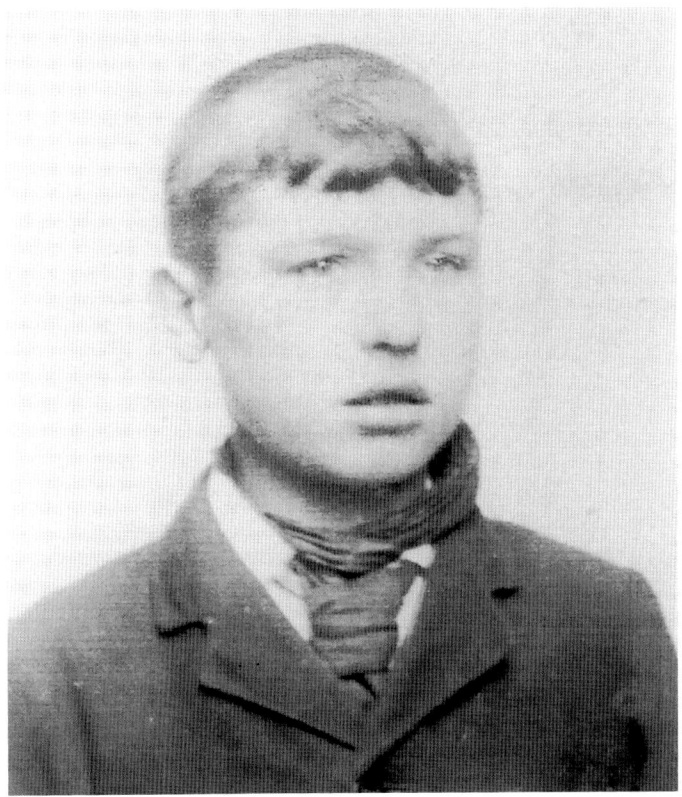

48. Henry Johnson, the lad with the choirboy looks, received six strokes of the birch at the age of 12 in 1896 for stealing aerated water in Aston. Later sent to an industrial school. All signs indicated a life destined for crime and punishment.

49. David Taylor. As a 13-year-old he stole a gun and never looked back. He spent most of his early life in institutions - reform school or prison. A prime candidate for the 'Peaky Blinders'.

The boys come into the school ignorant, abject, wretched with no aim in life, many of them never having had a word of kindness or a decent home. Mixing with the trained scholars, sufficiently fed and clothed, they became altogether different creatures, mentally and physically and soon began to take pleasure both in their work and in their school duties.

Many ex-inmates were encouraged to emigrate and some made good. They were at least taught to read and write and school authorities kept letters from all corners of the globe sent by their former charges. The following correspondence was delivered to Saltley reformatory from Australia in 1864. It has been abridged here for convenience:-

Dear M,
We had a very favourable voyage but not quite as quick as we should have liked...First, one of the sailors was drowned, and a life-boat went down with him: that was when we were in the Bay of Biscay. We were rolling about three days and nights; but at last we had a fair wind, and sailed away for the money-making land – which we thought – but I am sorry to say I found it quite different when I arrived, for there was plenty of work, but little money, though plenty to eat and drink. The meat is only 2d. per lb, as good meat as ever we eat, and plenty of bread and vegetables. But I am running away from my voyage...

Well we had good weather till we came to the Cape; there it was cold, but we soon got clear of all that. Then that was about half way. Oh! we were very tired, in fact sick, of the sea; for we could only see the same thing over and over again, every day...

We soon sighted Sydney Heads; the pilot came on board; took us in. No one was allowed to go ashore, not even the captain or the doctor, and we were set apart from all the other ships. That is the way with all the emigrant ships when they come into harbour, so that if there is any sickness on board the people in the city should not catch it...

At last we got leave to land, those that liked and those that didn't like could be hired off the ship; so as no one came on board for me I hired myself as farm labourer to Mr. H. M_ _ _ , for £15 a year, board, lodging, washing and mending. This is about one hundred miles up the country, out of Sydney, and I am quite happy. I get plenty to eat and drink, fruit if I want it, and a pony to ride every night when I have done my work. My chief work is driving bullocks, and I like my place, but it is very little money, and for only one year. I was hired from the ship on the 25th January 1864, and I am bound to stop one year, and do my best to satisfy my master and mistress. There is one more thing I must tell you. I spent a very miserable Christmas on board the ship. I did not even get a bit of bread, but plenty of hard biscuits, which if you hit them against the wall you could not break them, they were so hard. But I have got over all that now. I have plenty of good fresh meat and bread, and plenty of apricots...

I must now conclude with my best love to all inquiring friends, and accept the same yourself, from

Your affectionate W.Q.

50. In 1872, just one month after a flogging for the theft of five shillings, James Lee of William Street, together with two accomplices, stopped a baker's boy in Cumberland Street and relieved him of his cakes. More in hope rather than the expectation of his turning over a new leaf, the magistrate sentenced young James to one month's hard labour followed by five years in a reformatory.

Those who avoided this backdoor transportation were a positive menace on the streets. While 1870s Liverpool and Manchester had their 'scuttlers' and 'sloggers', Birmingham's gangs were named after the streets they infested. The Suffolk Street Gang and Livery Street Gang (with its equal opportunities policy) roamed the streets of their neighbourhoods seeking out vulnerable pedestrians. They mercilessly lashed their prey with belt buckles and *loaded guts* a length of sinew weighted with lead. Robbery was one motive but they appeared to seek confrontation for the kicks as well. If no strangers were handy at throwing out time the gangs would set about each other.

The fair folk of Birmingham sought to avoid direct routes to Edgbaston and Handsworth as many of the streets from town were virtually no-go areas, ruled by gangs of street-roughs described in the local paper as having *'low brows, evil eyes, vicious mouths, bullet heads and an unkempt appearance'*.

In 1870 a judge addressed four young men in the dock, his harsh words would probably be applauded in most courtrooms today:

> You have all of you been found guilty of robberies with violence on the streets of Birmingham. You have not only deprived persons of their property but have treated them with great violence. Now we have had eight cases of this nature at the Assizes and all of them occurred on the streets of Birmingham.
>
> This sort of thing must be stopped, if it can be stopped, because, notwithstanding the vigilance of the police, it really seems as though Birmingham was not a safe place to walk about in after a certain hour of the night. The law authorises me, in cases of this nature, not only to inflict the punishment of imprisonment but to direct the offender to be whipped. Now I intend that you and persons like you shall know that if you rob you will be imprisoned, and if in addition to that, you ill-treat those whom you rob, you will be whipped.
>
> It is right that if you inflict pain on others you should be made to feel pain yourselves. The sentence of the court upon you is that each of you be imprisoned with hard labour for eighteen calendar months and that in addition each receive twenty lashes with an instrument called a 'cat'.

The prisoners, who displayed a great dislike for the latter portion of the Judge's summation, were promptly removed.

52. 16-year-old William Yates could be in the cast of 'Oliver' today. Convicted in 1873 for vagrancy and in '74 for stealing 20lbs. of pig iron, a third 'simple larceny' saw the young man sent down for six months.

TWO LOST SOULS

One young man who didn't make the journey overseas was James Clifford, a lad in desperate need of the love of a good woman.

James Clifford, alias Shaw, following early parental rejection, joined with others of a similar background in a spectacularly unsuccessful life of crime. The lives of children born to unloving parents followed a repetitiously similar pattern.

Born in 1884, (in the photo on page 44 he is 18) he was discovered wandering the frozen streets of Birmingham as a 9-year-old in January 1893. Considered to be not *under proper guardianship*, James was shunted off to Shustoke Industrial school, his first taste of institutionalisation.

After being found not guilty on two previous appearances in court, Clifford's luck ran out in March 1897 when he was convicted of attempting to steal twelve stockings from a drapers on Steelhouse Lane. Two months hard labour seemed little deterrent, as, a month after release, he was running with a gang that smashed a window of a tobacconist's shop and ran off with 105 cigars and thirty packets of cigarettes. Four

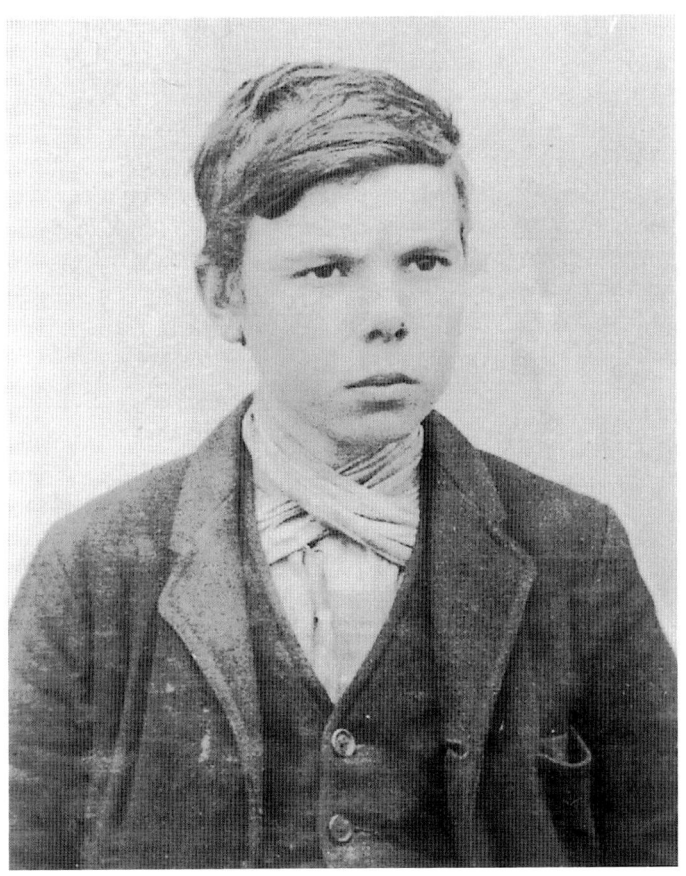

51. Another good-looking boy lured by a life of crime. 15-year-old William Middleton was convicted of stealing goods and money in 1902.

53. James Shaw, disowned by his parents. The only real 'affection' and acceptance he knew came from his peers.

months later, just before Christmas, James was released. Not surprisingly, his next two convictions (six weeks in all) were for sleeping out. He was probably quite pleased to be back in the comparative comfort of a warm cell. Indeed, on the very day of his subsequent release, he was re-arrested for gaming and later imprisoned for stealing pigs and puddings.

During one of his brief spells of liberty, the vulnerable young man was taken to a tattooist, where the rather unoriginal legend 'True Love' was permanently plastered beside a female hand, a heart, a couple of flowers and a collection of girls. What James needed was the real true love of a good woman. What he got was the company of strangers, in the shape of fellow thieves destined to spend their lives behind bars.

His next arrest, in April 1900, followed a raid on a clothes shop where once again the gang of four gained entry by smashing a window. This time, one of the boys carried a loaded six shooter. Clearly, the young offenders were now thoroughly hardened criminals who *did no work and lived by plunder* and predictably their sentences were going up. As the boys were sent down on this occasion, James for eight months, one of them pointed at the arresting officer and shouted: *I'll shoot him when I come out. I'll shoot him as sure as I'm going down these steps.*

He was encouraged by a woman's voice from the gallery: *Cheer up! Yes, do it!*

The next two years saw longer and longer sentences imposed upon our hero, for offences such as burglary and the theft of boots. He was also periodically fined for gambling. We will leave James as an 18-year-old, standing straight at 5′ 3″ looking ahead at a life in prison, looking back at a mere two years of liberty from the age of nine.

Give me a child until he is 7 and I will show you the man.

Or, indeed, the woman.

Agnes Gordon was born in 1883 and first apprehended sixteen years later. She had as unsuccessful a criminal career as James:

DATE	CHARGE	SENTENCE
08.11.99	Attempting to steal by trick one tin of milk worth 1s. 9d.	Discharged
16.07.00	Stealing sovereign	6 weeks H.L.
24.09.00	Using obscene language	Fine 5s.
03.04.01	Stealing boots	2 months H.L.
02.07.01	Stealing collars	3 months H.L.
16.01.02	Stealing fur necklet (Is the evidence in the photo?)	3 months H.L.
25.07.02	Stealing flowers	3 months H.L.
14.01.03	Attempt to obtain by means of false pretences 1s.11d.	3 months H.L.
14.01.03	Obtaining by false pretences 1s.7d.	3 months H.L.

54. There seemed little hope for Agnes Gordon who appeared to get caught at everything she tried

Not all offences were reported in the local press. Details of one of the above offences were, however, printed and it appears young Agnes was a very naughty girl indeed.

Agnes Gordon, 17, solderer of Sunny Mount, Tower Street was charged with stealing a sovereign from a little girl named Parry of Guilford Street on 14th July 1900. The child had been sent with the money to a pawnshop in Wheeler Street to redeem a pledge. She was robbed on the premises by the prisoner, who snatched the money and ticket out of Miss Parry's hand and fled. Superintendent Hannah said he had reason to believe Agnes was the same person who had lately robbed several children in a similar manner.

'FRESH FROM BRAWLING COURTS'

55. 61-year-old Mary Adey probably knew more about police procedure than the young man noting down her details. In 1898 Mary, along with an accomplice, pleaded guilty to picking pockets at New Street Station. Detective Sergeant Hefferman told the court that Mary was a renowned 'travelling thief'. She would certainly have been able to contribute to any 'good gaol guide' having been confined in several of Her Majesty's finest. Mary was sentenced to pass the whole of 1898 at hard labour in Winson Green.

Offenders came in all shapes and sizes with their outstanding peculiarities generally being noted down by the police for future identification. Among the features noted were:

> *varicose veins, weak eyes, bandy legs, pock marks on face, pimply face, three vaccination marks, very full under eyes; fleshy mole left of stomach; thick ear (left); large nose.*

These distinguishing marks were of course used to describe several different prisoners, not just one unfortunate.

56. The list of Jennie Willock's distinguishing marks was brutally honest: Pimply, missing two fingers off right hand: missing middle finger of left hand. In the late 1890s Jennie was fined for stealing boots

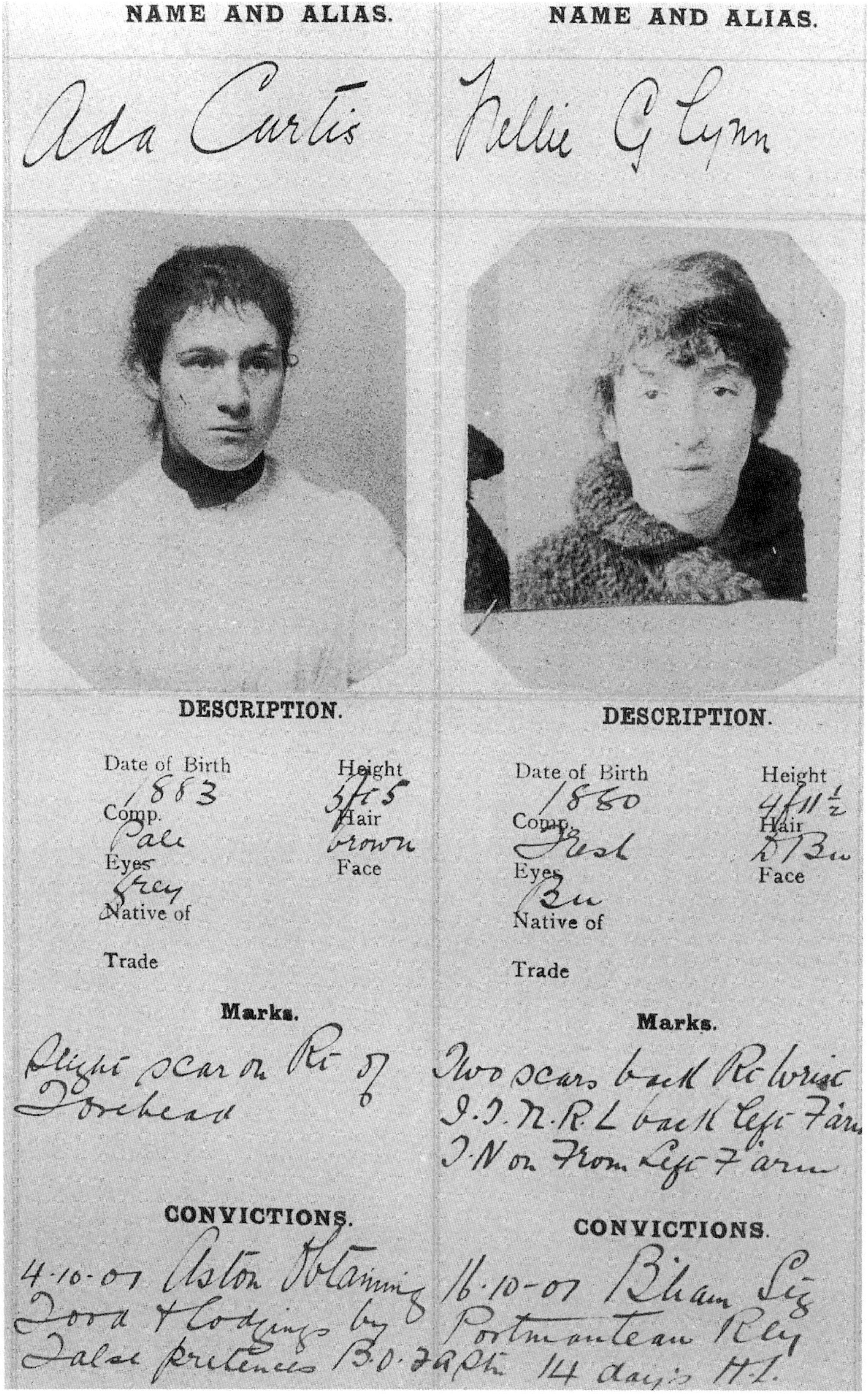

NAME AND ALIAS.	NAME AND ALIAS.
Ada Curtis	Nellie Glynn

DESCRIPTION.		DESCRIPTION.	
Date of Birth 1883	Height 5ft 5	Date of Birth 1880	Height 4ft 11½
Comp. Pale	Hair Brown	Comp. Fresh	Hair D Bn
Eyes Grey	Face	Eyes Bn	Face
Native of		Native of	
Trade		Trade	

Marks.

Slight scar on Rt of forehead

Marks.

Two scars back Rt wrist
J.J.N.R.L back Left F arm
J.N on Front Left F arm

CONVICTIONS.

4.10.01 Aston Obtaining food & lodgings by false pretences B.O. 7apth

CONVICTIONS.

16.10.01 B'ham Sess
Portmanteau Rly
14 days H.L.

57. What did the letters tattooed on Nellie's wrist stand for?

NAME AND ALIAS.	NAME AND ALIAS.
Thomas Redding @ Pat Carney & Swasbrook	Henry Lucas

DESCRIPTION.

Date of Birth: 1881
Height: 5/11
Comp.: Fair
Hair: Dk Bro
Eyes: Blue
Face:
Native of:
Trade:

DESCRIPTION.

Date of Birth: 1870
Height: 5/9½
Comp.: Dark
Hair: Dk Bro
Eyes: Grey
Face:
Native of:
Trade:

Marks.

Cross flags inside Lt forearm. Tryphan in Scroll outside Lt forearm. Crucifix & Anchor inside Rt forearm. LOVE outside right forearm.

Marks.

Small mole right side of breast. Abscess mk left jaw. Half circle tattooed on Left forearm.

CONVICTIONS.

B'ham 30.4.96 Stg Brushes Discharged
2.7.96 Sleeping out Dis
3.9.96 Stg Shovel 10/- or 14 Days
19.11.96 Obstruction 5/-
16.9.97 Stg money 1 month HL
2.3.98 Stg Ham 2 month HL
5.10.98 Shopbreaking 6 mths HL
14.6.99 hot ringing bell on Cycle 5/- or 7 Days HL
29.7.99 Obs. lang & assault on PC 10/- & Costs or 14 Days
Cov. "99 Burglary 4 yrs PS
Aston 15.4.03 PC ast 12 mths HL

CONVICTIONS.

Sutton Coldfield 28.4.91 Trespassing in search of game 5/ & Costs 8/6
" 15.9.91 Similar offence 40/- & Costs 13/6
Aston 22.5.03 Stg blue Ducks 6 mths HL

58. Details as to the appearance of prisoners and their identification marks were noted for future reference. Offenders unwittingly helped police with their predilection for rather unimaginative tattoos. Thomas Redding's arms were decorated with LOVE and a crucifix yet he certainly didn't love his neighbour, being convicted for assault, obscene language and burglary. Henry Lucas was a professional poacher.

 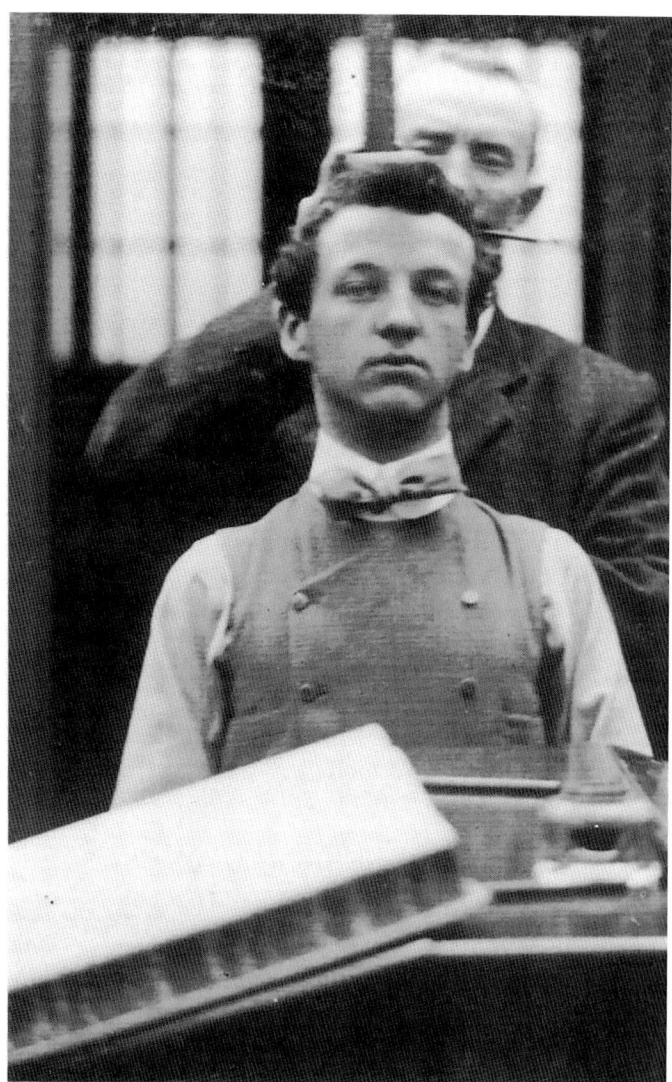

59. Details of prisoners being noted in the summer of 1904. Henry Harris (on the left) refused to give his address. He was referred to as 'a dangerous man' by Superintendent Daniel. Arrested under the Prevention of Crimes act, he was spotted 'tapping ladies pockets'. Harris was sent down for ten months. Newspaper reports name the man on the right as John Gardiner. In police record books he is John Goodwin. He was a little more co-operative and did divulge his address in Highfield Place, Anderton Street. Gardiner/Goodwin was charged with loitering but found not guilty.

Many offenders were known by both police and public alike by their nicknames. As today these were derived from a number of sources – a person's character, their physical characteristics, where they come from, their job etc. etc. Amongst those serving time in Winson Green in the nineteenth century were *Cheeky Charlie, Jockey Logan, Bristol Bill, Tommy the Knuckler, Cabbage Green, Comical Lil, The Old Hag, Ribs, Daddy and Brains*. It's probably as well not to delve too deeply into the derivation of the nicknames of two more characters. *Stiff Dick* was probably as popular as *Edward Shitehouse* was friendless.

A brief description as to different offenders' *modus operandi* might be noted. Mary Smith would call for drinks knowing she had no money to pay the bill. Elizabeth Thompson would feign insanity in order to gain admission to hospital. Numerous other recidivists were listed, in what sounds like a commendation, as *good pickpockets*.

Typical headlines from just one day's court reports include:

Stealing sausages
A dishonest domestic
The 'muchly married' wife case
A dishonest charwoman
Stealing a piece of pork

Watches were the main targets of dips but literally nothing was safe. In just one day's proceedings magistrates had to deal with thefts of the following items, presented in the order in which they came to court: a shovel, a spade, a bricklayer's jacket, 100 cigars, hooves and marrow bones, bedsteads, horse clippers, 8lbs. of horse hair, a pair of driving reins, six brushes, sheets from lodgings, thirteen bunches of onions, one pipe, nine rabbits, candles, four bottles of porter, oats, a bag of oysters, one pork pie, ginger beer, a pig's head, seven papers from a mail lad and a quantity of goat flesh from a slaughterhouse.

During this period in Birmingham, one could be prosecuted for riding a cycle furiously – between 10 and 15 m.p.h. – ringing the changes, putting a boy up the chimney instead of a machine, wandering abroad and frequenting. A butcher was prosecuted for having 10lbs of decomposing sausages. In an effort to demonstrate their quality he even went so far as to eat one in front of the inspector. Now, where have we seen that before?

60. In and out of prison on a number of drink-related charges, Ellen Jackson's life is detailed in her C.V.

PIE-EYED AND LEGLESS

Mary Ann Glover chalked up her fiftieth appearance in court in November 1871. The 35-year-old pleaded that she had only downed two half-pints and could not possibly be drunk and incapable. Perhaps in a gesture to mark her half-century the judge took pity on her and she was discharged.

A year later, however, Mary made her fifty-third appearance, in a somewhat befuddled state of mind, having somehow aged five years in the intervening twelve months. Alcohol does indeed speed up the aging process! Mary had been arrested, pie-eyed and legless, outside a brothel in Severn Street. A crowd had gathered, some of whom amused themselves by drawing on her face with fingers dipped in soot.

When informed that this was her fifty-third appearance Mary, to the general amusement of the court, pleaded that she had had an 'overdose' of Champagne. She went on to tell the court that she'd been on a spree with two young men who had forced her to drink against her better judgment. Mr. Manton, the magistrate, said that it was useless sending her to prison. Advising her to go to the workhouse he discharged the dipso, who probably went to a *public house*.

Mary Ann almost certainly quaffed a jug or two with Ellen Jackson. Ellen seems to have spent just enough time outside gaol to celebrate release by getting tanked and re-arrested.

THE CRIMINAL RECORD OF ELLEN JACKSON
SEPTEMBER 1871 – DECEMBER 1872

AGE: 47 HEIGHT: 5' 3" COMPLEXION: SALLOW
ADDRESS: BACK OF BUCK ROAD, BIRMINGHAM.
PROFESSION: SEAMSTRESS
MARITAL STATUS: MARRIED

Scar over left eye. Mole on back. Lost upper tooth. Vaccination marks. Ears pierced.

DATE	OFFENCE	SENTENCE
18.09.71	Drunk and riotous	7 days
31.10.71	Wilful damage	1 month H.L.
17.01.72	Obscene language	14 days
17.02.72	Drunk and riotous	1 month
18.03.72	Want of status	6 weeks
29.04.72	Drunk and riotous	1 month
05.09.72	Drunk and riotous	14 days
02.11.72	Drunk and riotous	14 days
16.11.72	Drunk and riotous	1 month
16.12.72	Simple larceny	3 months

For Ellen, 1872 was a vintage year.

BRIDGET LYONS AGAIN

Another familiar in Brum's Streets and broadsheets was 50-year-old Bridget Lyons. *A woman of ill-fame*, she was arrested in May 1890 in Newton Row. Bridget vehemently denied the charge of being drunk and disorderly, insisting that she was 'a crucified woman' and the wife of a sergeant armourer.

When the stipendiary asked, *What's known of her?* the weary reply from Inspector Hall greatly amused all present: *Almost everything, Sir, this is her fortieth appearance.*

Bridget was having none of this and screamed from the dock: *You're a fibber, Hall.* The inspector went on to relate that 'the ladies' had spent a good deal of money trying to reclaim the woman but it was no good. Bridget spent the next month inside.

The ladies referred to were the 'Ladies for the Care of Friendless Girls' who tried, with varying degrees of success, to reform drunken women. Bridget was obviously beyond help but there were some success stories. In 1904 the local paper reported that at one meeting a reformed alcoholic had recited the whole of Tennyson's 'Lady of Shallot' without mistakes.

Drunken women were periodically rounded up and taken to a lockup to sleep off the effects of a gin or two too many. Mary Ann James, of no fixed abode, was found flat on her back in the Aston road at one o' clock on a Saturday morning in 1890. She was hauled before the beak on charges of drunkenness:

MAGISTRATE'S CLERK: *How was it that you got drunk?*
MARY JAMES: *Because the policeman took my lodging money from me.*

The policeman curtly denied the accusation and insisted that Mary had drunk two doses of tincture of rhubarb.

MAGISTRATE'S CLERK: *How have you come into this wretched condition?*

MARY JAMES: *Because I married a Welsh clergyman – a rogue and a vagabond.*

MAGISTRATE'S CLERK: *You must pay five shillings or three days imprisonment.*

MARY JAMES: *Five shillings indeed! I only had threepence and that the officer took from me.*

On May 3rd 1900, 42-year-old Sarah Massey notched up her 112th conviction. She was found guilty of 'burglariously entering' the house of Alfred Kane and stealing ten fur 'necklets'. Sarah behaved strangely and threatened to break every window in Mr Kane's premises at Gooch Street, *that she would have some clothing to wear.*

The judge considered she was not of sound mind and sentenced her to twelve months inside *so that she may be in safe custody.*

THIS COUNTRY IS TRULY RURAL

Before the days of the breathalyser some naive tests were used to 'prove' a prisoner drunk or sober. Suspect drunkards were asked to balance on one leg and then the other and then asked to walk up and down the hall. In the 1890s this procedure was followed by the Sir William Lawson Test, which required suspects to repeat the following sentence without slurring or confusing the words. If you've had a couple of bevvies before reading this – and who can blame you? – you might care to repeat the following:- 'The British Constitution is a truly noble institution.'

Besides being difficult to say, the statement was a complete lie.

It's worth repeating that no woman had the right to vote until after World War One and in court both judge and jury were composed entirely of males. For the most part women came to court as victims or as petty criminals charged with minor offences.

In one particular case, which came before the magistrate towards the end of the century a prosecuting officer was asked whether the accused had repeated the expression 'this country is truly rural'. When told he had not, the magistrate asked if the prisoner had been instructed to 'walk the plank'. When a second 'no' was forthcoming, the policeman added that he had asked him to walk down the steps of his house, which in his opinion was the more difficult thing. The magistrate tried a third time: *'Did he smell of beer?'* The P.C., wearying of the case replied:

'I have a great objection to putting my nose in another person's mouth.'

The case was dismissed.

Time for a drink?

One of Birmingham's more renowned characters was Thomas Larvin, popularly known as 'Thomas Tank'. Tommy was so well-known he had a regular spot in the local paper. A typical entry, dated 31st October 1904 reads:

A MONTH'S SOBRIETY GUARANTEED

Thomas Larvin otherwise 'Thomas Tank' made his 118th appearance. On Friday night P.C. Barker saw Tommy in Corporation Street in a state of drunkenness and assuming a fighting attitude to passers-by. Inspector Hall remarked that the prisoner was before the stipendiary a few days ago and pleaded so hard that he was given another chance. The magistrate's clerk said the prisoner was absolutely hopeless adding 'He ought to be sent to an asylum I should think.'

Larvin, who had nothing to say for himself, was sent down for one month.

Tommy (the)Tank(ed-up Engine) fought what the police optimistically viewed as his last battle in Birmingham Police Court on March 23rd. 1907. The habitual offender had chalked up 140 previous convictions. The straw that broke the magistrate's back came when Tommy popped in for a bevvy in the George and Dragon in Steelhouse Lane. Being refused service he picked up a stone ginger beer bottle and threw it at the the barman with *'a force that might have killed him'*.

Tommy was a danger to himself and anyone who came into contact with him. This time he was confined indefinitely to Winson Green Asylum.

HANGING OUT IN SUMMER LANE

On December 16th 1872 Joseph Cotterell, of 50 Summer Lane, was charged with being drunk and indecently exposing himself in Woodcock Street. He had 27 previous convictions for the same offence.

There seems to have been something in the water in Summer Lane. The previous year 25-year-old Stephen Moore, who lived three doors down from Joseph Cotterell, was charged with the same offence. Had the men known about each other's inclinations they might have hung out together, instead of offending the gentle souls of Birmingham.

There was something about railway stations and carriages that turned men into exhibitionists. Moore exposed himself to Mary Anne Whitehouse in a third class carriage on the London and North West Railway. Details of the offence, plus a little sideswipe at the railways for having the wrong kind of communication cord, were reported in the local paper:

Directly after passing Edgbaston Station the prisoner indecently exposed himself; and the girl, who was the only person in the carriage put her head out of the window and screamed for assistance…The cord which should have communicated with the guard or engineer had previously been pulled, but, as one witness remarked 'with no effect – as usual.'

The quick flash resulted in Moore picking oakum for three months.

PORTRAIT AND DESCRIPTION OF HABITUAL DRUNKARD.

Register No. (b)

Name and Alias— Thomas Larwin, "Tommy Tank"

Residence— No home

Place of Business or where employed— None

Age— 50

Height— 5 feet 1 inch

Build— Slim

Complexion— Fresh

Hair— Brown

Eyes— Brown

Whiskers—

Moustache— Brown

Shape of nose— Short

Shape of face— Thin Broad Forehead

Peculiarities or marks— Cut scar down left of forehead near temple. Scar Bridge of nose mole right cheek large cut scar right upper arm.

Profession or occupation— Hawker

Date and nature of Conviction— 16th January 1903 Drunk on Licensed Premises, 10s + costs, or 14 days hard labour.

Court at which convicted— Birmingham City Police Court.

61. Tommy Tank (like his more famous namesake, a son of the city) had well over 100 drink related offences and was Birmingham's most famous inebriate. Tommy left a trail of destruction behind and to the relief of the beer drinking public, and for his own protection, was confined to Winson Green asylum in 1907. He must have been released, though, because in July 1998 a Miss Sly (89) recalled as a child witnessing Tommy in action. On that occasion, with one vicious swipe of his walking stick, Tommy cleared the bar of all the beer and glasses.

62. The mad, the sad and the bad. Thomas Larvin, scourge of publicans.

63. Charles Bradley. What could you do with a lad who refused to work in a workhouse? He was sent to prison for seven days

64. James Smith, a tearaway, who from his expression, is not too appreciative of the attention he's receiving at the hands of the police.

65. After snatching watches, farmer Northbrook pushed a plucky assistant through a plate-glass window. Along with time-pieces, boots were probably the most popular targets of thieves.

GRAB AND SMASH

Farmer Northbrook planned the job meticulously. His hidden weapon weighed heavily in his pocket; his heartbeat raced. 'Keep calm', he kept telling himself 'keep calm' as he entered the jewellers in High Street. Feigning interest in the delicate trinkets on show, he glanced furtively around the shop then, reaching deeply into his pocket, Northbrook brought out his weapon.

The technological age had not yet reached the farmer's particular neck of the woods. Producing a stone wrapped in a large pocket handkerchief he laid it menacingly onto the counter. As Northbrook's large hands greedily scooped up a set of valuable gold watches, the far from menaced young assistant had a go. Vaulting the counter he grappled with the thick-set agriculturalist. A few years behind a jeweller's counter were no match for ten in the field, however; Northbrook simply picked the plucky assistant up, as if he were a bale of hay, and tossed him through the window. The sound of breaking glass reached the police, who clocked up a remarkable response time, arresting the rural rascal before he could effect his escape

A BAD GIRL

In 1884 Harriet Hollins, a bad girl, was charged with obtaining several pounds by means of false pretences. The precocious 18-year-old acquired money by pretending her hand had been amputated owing to the negligence of her employer. Harriet would shuffle around with her arm bound up and for good measure had her foot bandaged too.

For five months Harriet did the rounds, telling a tale of how she had lost her hand at the works of Mr. Frank Heath of Leopold Street. She even had a list printed out which she thrust into the hands of prospective sympathisers. It read: 'A list of subscriptions for the benefit of Harriet Hollins.' The roll featured names such as Reverend P. Reynolds, Vicar of St Stevens and listed his contribution of ten shillings.

Harriet pestered anyone and everyone who looked as if they had a bob or two, silently handing them the card to elicit donations. In court the magistrate's clerk asked Inspector Hall to examine the prisoner. Hands and feet were all present and correct.

Harriet's father told the court that he had not seen her for the previous three months. He knew where she'd be for the next three when the magistrate passed his sentence, adding: *'you are a bad girl'*.

Offending has no upper age limit. In 1872, the 72-year-old Philip Evans, cabinet maker, was charged with stealing a Windsor chair, belonging to a Mrs. Wylete, from the market hall. The prisoner was on remand for reports concerning his character. Police Constable Lathan said that he had interviewed the prisoner's son who, in a rather neat reversal of roles, told Lathan that he could do nothing with his father. When the younger Evans had looked after his father, the old man had frequently stolen from him. The prisoner certainly had previous convictions. Magistrate Kynnersley was reluctant to send such an old man to prison, but as there was no more suitable place for him to go, Philip Evans was sent down for one month.

66. A rare photograph of a man born in the eighteenth century. As a 6-year-old Philip Evans joined in the celebrations following Nelson's victory at the Battle of Trafalgar. In later life he became very confused and was charged with stealing a Windsor chair. The question is: was he wearing a wig?

A SQUEEZE OF BLUE

Altercations between slum dwellers were inevitable. On 15th July 1884 Selina Corcoron, an Irishwoman, as her name suggests, appeared in the dock with a piece of bread in one hand and a jug in the other. Whether she had not quite finished her breakfast, wanted to sample prison fare or intended to give holy communion, is not recorded. Selina was charged with assaulting a neighbour, Mary Ann Toy, and with throwing a bucket of washing water over her.

The prisoner gave a long incoherent statement, the gist of which was that the complainant, Mary Ann Toy, had approached her in the washroom with the request:

Mrs. Corcoron, have you got a squeeze of blue in your bag?

Mrs. Corcoron, assuming her neighbour to be short of funds, duly supplied the *'squeeze of blue'* before continuing with the wash. A short time later she saw Mary Toy boldly produce money for other items. Dazed with shock, the generous Mrs C realised that she'd been conned. A swift 'marmer' to the mouth settled the debt as far as she was concerned, but the tide turned against her. Not to be trifled with, Mrs Toy decided to press charges. When the matter finally surfaced in court, Mrs Corcoron was fined one shilling.

Given the nature of the people they were dealing with, court officials, witnesses and the police were often in the firing line. Abuse didn't just take the form of verbal threats but also included the occasional episode of physical assault.

Many prisoners and witnesses appeared before the court a wee bit worse for wear, their heads swathed in bandages and brains well pickled with alcohol. The lives of judges, the police and hostile witnesses were regularly threatened in final acts of defiance.

Religious zealots were sometimes tried for interrupting services. They also interrupted trials and held the court in contempt, making it clear that they only answered to a higher court. One such Bible basher confronted a judge as follows:

You are a liar. May the Lord strike you dead like he did Ananias and Sapphira.

(Acts V for original)

BREAD AND WATER

In 1871 Eliza Davis, a domestic servant, described in the local rag as a *virago*, was convicted of stealing a quantity of plate and a pair of gold bracelets. As the nineteen-year-old was about to be removed from the dock she broke into a rapid volley of abusive and filthy language. She then drew a large crust of dry bread from her pocket and correctly aimed it at the detective's head. She then spat at him. Thus furnished with a taste of prisoner's fare, Detective Beckley stated that Eliza had been very violent when he had taken her into custody. Eliza was immediately charged with assaulting an officer and committed for a further six weeks. She left the court screaming more threats and obscenities at Beckley.

On 15th March 1872 P.C. McCrohon was about to give his evidence...*'I was proceeding in a northerly direc...'* when he was struck a severe blow on the side of the face. Marie Allport, a forty-year-old prostitute, had taken advantage of the policeman's proximity to exact a little revenge. Shaken, but not stirred, the policeman continued his evidence against the woman from Clement Street. When found guilty of soliciting she threatened in no uncertain terms to thrash him when she was walking the streets again. Gesticulating wildly, and shouting abuse and threats to the police and magistrates, Marie was ushered to prison, where she was guaranteed a heroine's welcome from the unfortunate sisterhood.

67. James Farmer was rather partial to the odd scrap and would attack anyone he thought was looking at him.

STRONG IN THE ARM...

James Farmer was one of those men you dread encountering in pubs, the lonesome loser who believes everyone is looking at him. Strong in the arm, but weak in the head, Farmer was quite simply a nasty bully. With none of today's magic pills or psychiatrists to help him, the 26-year-old was a real danger, both to himself and anybody who (he thought) crossed him...or looked at him!

Farmer was one of the hardest cases in Birmingham. In and out of gaol, he assaulted warders and policemen alternately and had been flogged so many times that he appeared impervious to the punishment. Farmer often threatened that he would be hung for the murder of a screw or copper.

On 16th June 1890 the burly bully stood in court, charged with assaulting Bridget Cohen. Seething with pent up rage, muttering under his breath, the whole world against him again, Farmer bided his time.

As was his wont, Farmer had given his victim a hefty kick in the gut. When asked to explain his actions the prisoner told the court that the woman was 'as black as a crow.' His only regret was that he had not kicked her enough. He argued that she deserved the assault as, a few months previously, she had sought assistance when he threw one of his boots at a bobby.

As the judge passed sentence of two months hard labour, the bully saw red. He swiftly vaulted the dock, landing on his solicitor's table. Focused wild eyes on Detective Price, Farmer ran along the table and directed a kick at Price's face. Fortunately he missed, because the terrific speed of the action, combined with the weight of the heavily-nailed boot, would surely have ended the policeman's career. Frustrated by his failure, the prisoner spun towards the judge and like an angry bull, casting all aside, he bore down upon the subject of his rage. It needed five policemen to throw him on his back and remove those deadly weapons, his awful boots. The public was thrilled by this act of defiance and crowded the bench in an effort to get a better view.

Some semblance of calm was restored when Farmer was manacled in the dock, whereupon he was summarily sentenced to a further two months for assaulting Price. As he was taken down, he gave vent to a final stream of abuse, concluding with the words: *What the ____ do I care for you.*

One can only guess as to how pleased the warders were to have their old friend back again.

A couple of weeks before Christmas 1911, the hawker Thomas Field stood in the dock charged with stealing boots from a pawnbroker's shop in Green Lane. Field sensed which way the wind was blowing, as the trial drifted towards its conclusion. Seizing the stool provided for his comfort, Field hurled it with startling swiftness. He hit the judge smack in the face, dislodging both wig and pince-nez., to which his lordship calmly responded: *I am hurt*.

The judge was assisted from the bench, to return minutes later sporting a shiner. Good humouredly he advised the dock officers:*Take care he doesn't throw another thing like that. He might kill me next time.*

In the nearest thing to an apology, Field said that he had meant the stool to hit the witness, D.I. Moxon, whom he proceeded to threaten. Given the very long sentence of five years and with no more ammunition to hand, the prisoner contented himself with a few choice curses – this time aimed at the beak.

ALL EARS

When the ale starts flowing the bets get going.

How many wagers have been struck under the influence and never paid out when sober? In August 1884 a group of four drinking cronies began an argument as to who was the fastest runner. A drunken challenge was laid down by 32-year-old Edward Millward and taken up by the equally inebriated Thomas Tranter. The loser was liable to pay for half a gallon of ale for the quartet. Tranter won at a trot, but Millward was a bad loser and would not pay up. Instead, he took the chance to sneak away but was spotted and dogged by his thirsty companions. They followed the welcher to Lower Brearely Street where their dispute became so heated that a woman passer-by treated them all to a beer.

The men duly returned to their local in the aptly named Hospital Street when all hell was let loose a second time. Mike Tyson is far from being the first person to sample human flesh. After Millward set about his friends they were forced to appear in court minus large portions of their ears.

Having lost the bet, but won the fight, Millward's prize was a six month's sentence.

ON THE BUSES

The term 'job's worth' is a new one but over-zealous and unimaginative workers have been with us for centuries. On 31st May, 1896 37-year-old James Hall was taking a gamble. He boarded the tram in Great Hampton Street with a used ticket. Unfortunately for him a 42-year-old bus inspector, Richard Lewis, got on at the next stop and spotted the attempted fraud and promptly demanded the fare. The two men fell to bickering and finally to blows, battering each other as if their lives depended on the penny fare. Unfortunately the fare-dodger's did. The tragic Hall was knocked senseless and died in hospital the following morning. Richard Lewis was acquitted of a charge of manslaughter.

68. One of the few professional men to come before the courts. Henry Parry wrote threatening letters to a fellow solicitor promising to 'send a release in the shape of a bullet through your_____ carcass'.

HATRED IS INVETERATE ANGER

Forgive and forget is a far better policy than a lifetime bent on revenge.

Henry Parry, a former Birmingham solicitor, became hell bent on destroying another solicitor's career and, if this failed, that same solicitor's life.

The object of his hatred was a Mr. G. Johnson, the executor of Parry senior's will. Parry was convinced that he had been swindled out of a great deal of money and he pointed the finger at his fellow lawyer. Having left Birmingham to live in Margate, Parry bombarded his perceived enemy with hundreds of letters listing his grievances.

On April 12th 1904 he wrote as follows:

I have your letter. The release I shan't send. I will be in Birmingham in a few days and shall send a release in the shape of a bullet through your _____ carcass and that of Baker for the way you have treated me.

Two months later he sent a postcard to Johnson that was considered (presumably by prying eyes?) to be so grossly offensive that the Post Office refused to deliver it!

I am leaving here for Birmingham tonight. You can arrange the internment with your undertaker.

Charged with sending threatening letters, Parry was sentenced to six months 'in the second division' – a punishment dreaded by all Blues fans.

A ZOOLOGICAL CONTROVERSY

Magistrates and court officials welcomed a little light relief from the never-ending round of domestic disputes and petty pilferings. Those offenders who could imbibe the amber nectar without resorting to fisticuffs often brightened up the day of court reporters, as the following examples demonstrate:

In April 1870 a 36-year-old brewer, Andrew Slater, was charged with being drunk and incapable of taking care of his *horse and trap* and with *furiously driving along Brook Street*. Slater, in his defence, said that the charge was wrong as he did not own a *horse and trap*. The arresting officer, a Police Constable Stephenson, then testified that he saw the defendant drunk with a *pony and trap*. Here Slater intervened:

SLATER: *It wasn't, it was a donkey (laughter).*
P.C.STEPHENSON: *It was a pony.*
CLERK: *Is there anyone else who saw the animal?*
P.C. STEPHENSON: *This man in the brown coat, Inspector Percy.*

Inspector Percy innocently gave his opinion that he believed the animal to be a *mule*. While the magistrate held his head in exasperation P.C. Stephenson continued his testimony: *I should call it a pony. The prisoner was unable to sit upright in the cart.*

Few of the spectators in court could sit upright either as the Pythonesque zoological debate continued. The prisoner was eventually found guilty of driving furiously and fined five shillings. No decision was reached as to which species of animal was being neglected.

In 1907 a carter Edward Jones popped into his local for a pint, leaving his horse unattended. When asked the silly question why he had left the horse unattended he gave the appropriate reply:

Because I could not take the horse in with me!

The magistrate had no sense of humour. Fine: five shillings.

EXCEEDINGLY DIRTY STOCKINGS

A year later John Goulding was charged with being drunk and attempting suicide. The 20-year-old surrendered himself to a policeman, insisting that he had committed a murder in Hagley Road four years previously. Not much credence was given to the confession but Goulding was escorted to Duke Street Police Station to spend a night in the cells on account of his intoxication. Here the prisoner manifested symptoms of lunacy, fighting his own shadow and indulging in set-to's with imaginary bloodthirsty foes.

When left alone he made a vain attempt at suicide by hanging himself with a pair of 'exceedingly dirty stockings' which he had pulled off his feet.

In court Goulding promised that he would not go mad again. He blamed his behaviour on an overindulgence of stimulating cordials. For the record, he also retracted his murder confession.

LAUGHTER IN COURT

Not all those charged were gormless, humourless oafs. One man, convicted of embezzlement, was obviously a frustrated thespian. When asked if he had anything to say for himself he turned to his audience and addressed them thus:-

Friends, Romans, Countrymen...

He then proceeded to recite the whole of Mark Anthony's oration on the death of Caesar and appeared genuinely surprised when the judge told him that his utterings made no difference whatsoever to the investigation.

A prison warder who served the best part of fifty years at Winson Green related several anecdotes in the *Mercury*. One of his favourite stories concerned two prisoners, an Irishman and a Scotsman, both of whom he accompanied to court. The Irishman was first in the dock. A short time later, sporting a large grin, he joined the prisoners below, having managed to obtain a fairly light sentence. The Scotsman was desperate to know how he'd managed to be treated so leniently. The Irishman explained:

I looked the judge in the face and I says – you old blackguard, ye sit there pretending to do justice and norra bit of justice do you ever do. If I had my way wid ye I'd send ye for twelve months to the treadmill to learn your manners and give ye a taste of the cat o' nine tails too ye scoundrel. To sit there sending innocent men to gaol, you ought to be in gaol yourself. You rogue, spalpeen, ye divil I'd give ye one over the head if only I had ye here a minit – and the judge he just looked up and he says six months...that's how to talk to him.

The Scot took him at his word, returning a short time later, barely able to control his temper. He was politely questioned by the Irishman:

– Well, did you let him have it?
– Let him have it! Ay and I did. What have ye to say his lairdship said and I began – ye blackguard, fool – when he stopped me. He said eighteen months and that's six months for contempt of court.
– But how did ye speak to him? Did ye shout it out boldly?
– Ay, ay I just spoke out at the top of my voice.
– That's where ye made the mistake. What I said to him I said under my breath.

CHOPSTICKS

Catherine Jones and her husband disagreed about the food of love. She believed it was music while her policeman husband put his faith in bread and cheese. In December 1899 Catherine, from 245, Heath Street, Winson Green contracted to pay ten shillings a month for the hire of a grand piano. She did not discuss the matter with her husband. In the many rows that followed he insisted they needed all his salary for food and other necessities of life (beer perhaps?). Catherine played on. Her husband seethed. After eighteen months the policeman took the law into his own hands, and, wielding an axe, played a new tune on the instrument to which it had not been adjusted (chopsticks, possibly?). The couple then had the nerve to attempt to return the instrument. The court found for the music shop and the pair were forced to pay the full cost of the instrument.

THE ITALIAN CONNECTION

In 1873 an 85-year-old Italian, a wily old fox, appeared before the court charged with begging. He had an ingenious defence. Charles Rabbiott was accused of wandering the streets of Birmingham with a tin plate in front of him asking for relief as he was blind. He was questioned by a Mr. Kynnersley:

– Why don't you go to the workhouse?
– I would sooner go to London (Laughter).
– If you don't go to the workhouse you must go to gaol.
– Well, you have me before you and you must please yourself.
– Do you belong to Birmingham?
– No, Sir. I belong to Italy, and have been in England about forty years. I have been blind three or four years. I never beg. I never ask for so much as a drop of water. I put this plate in front of me because it keeps me from hurting my stomach against a stump. (Laughter).

One nil to Italy. Promising to leave town the prisoner was discharged.

Organ grinding sounds a rather painful process but in the 1890s the trade was extremely lucrative. Thomas Biggins of 13, New Bartholomew Street regularly hired one such musical instrument but lacked the patience or charm of native Italian grinders. If spectators did not toss him a coin or two Biggins would threaten them with a large knife. When asked if he had anything to say in mitigation he replied:

I hope you will pity me. I am an orphan.

After being questioned as to his age the defendant replied that he was 25. In a sarcastic tone of voice the magistrate replied *'An orphan and only 25 years of age!'* He was then sentenced to one month inside.

Before the days of ice-cream wars, turf disputes over piano-grinder's pitches led to gang warfare. In 1893 Francesco Didunca and Silvestro Rossi were summoned for assaulting Cianghetto Martino and Antonio Tavolieri. The court was packed with tempestuous olive skinned families and harassed interpreters. Even the horses tethered outside were restless.

Accusations, in two languages, flew thick and fast. Tavolieri, speaking in Italian, swore that he'd met the two accused in 'a wide street for men' which, when translated, turned out to be the more prosaic Hagley Road. Marrtino and Tavolieri were informed, in unambiguous terms, that the terrain belonged to the

69. Landlords who refused to serve drunks were often targets for flying bottles and fists. Umbrellas were less common.

Rossis and had done so for thirteen years. If they did not pick up their hurdy-gurdy and get out of town fast they would have their throats slashed. At this crucial point, a loud whinny, from one of the horses, penetrated the silence of the court.

The tale continued. The Tavioleri's and Martino's had apparently stood their ground. Proud men, they were all too willing to fight for their families and the right to make music. Rossi unsheathed his knife, stabbed his mouthy opponent in the lip and proceeded to beat him with an iron bar. A full scale civil disturbance did not result in any clear cut winners.

Both parties were fined for the affray. This was surely just the opening round of a family saga destined to run and run.

Another Italian, Giaco Mantonio Fella, also relied on an interpreter in court. Prosecuted for being drunk and using obscene language, the police officer observed that when arrested he, (the Italian) swore in very good English. He was fined 2s. 6d.

THE DICE MEN

As opposed to positively promoting the lottery today, successive governments in the 1800s saw it as their job *to prevent the gullible and rash from wasting their money.* Top of their hit list were fortune-tellers and illegal bookies.

It seems astonishing nowadays, with legal betting shops dotted all over the city, that the police, until fairly recently, expended a great deal of time and energy preventing illegal gambling. What was above board for the landed gentry at racecourses was against the law for the working and criminal classes. Despite this, many pubs and working men's clubs catered for gambling mania.

These were often raided and frequently infiltrated by police in plain clothes. One of the earliest recorded raids was on a gambling club in Birchnall Street in 1863. Police quickly identified and collared the scout before moving in. A local reporter at the scene takes up the story:

One of the detectives tapped twice at the door, and this being the usual signal, it was at once opened. All the officers then rushed into the room, where between twenty and thirty people were standing round a square table. The room itself would be about 15 feet square…The only furniture in the room consisted of a couple of chairs, and a square table covered with ragged oil-cloth, around which all the gamblers were standing. There was only a solitary candle on the table, but as the fire burnt brightly, there was sufficient light to enable everything in the room to be seen clearly. Nearly every one was smoking a short pipe, and the heat and stench of the place was positively sickening. A pile of coppers was on the table, but the dicebox and dice had been thrown on the floor, and were picked up from under the table.

The master of the house, a big hulking fellow in his shirt-sleeves, smoking a scientifically-coloured clay pipe was for a time inclined to be insolent. Then he suddenly altered his tone, and said that he was a poor man, that he had been earning very little money lately, and that he was only raffling off a few pigeons. The statement did not do him much good, and he was hand-cuffed and taken to prison, every one in the house, having, in the meantime, been gently assisted to the door, where they received at the hands of the officers a reminder which quickened their steps and caused them to take their departure in a hasty and somewhat unceremonious manner.

The *big hulking fellow in shirt-sleeves* was sent down for three months.

ASSAULT ON A PEDESTRIAN

Pedestrian races held at Bingley Hall were amongst the most popular of entertainments in the 1880s. Competitors would circle the track for twelve hours – 11am. to 11pm – and those completing the most laps were pronounced the winners. In this primitive forerunner to Le Mans, competitors vied for the 'Sir John Astley's Championship Distance go-as-you please belt'.

There was international competition as long ago as 1882, with the inclusion in the fourteen strong field of the well-respected champion from the United States, Sam Day. One of the reasons the race was so popular was that it attracted huge wagers and thousands of pounds would go to the backers of the athlete with most stamina. Just over five hours and 44 miles into the race the leader was a man named Cartwright. He was one of the favourites and going well when a spectator rushed onto the track and dealt him a violent blow across the head with a heavy bludgeon. Blood flowed copiously for several minutes as the assailant, who had obviously wagered his money on a different competitor, outsprinted his pursuers.

It was thought that the injury would necessitate the competitor's withdrawal, but, encouraged by his friends, he carried on. A man was later arrested for the assault but there were serious doubts as to his culpability.

70. ASSAULT ON A PEDESTRIAN - BINGLEY HALL BIRMINGHAM.

Fortune Tellers and their Dupes at Birmingham.

71. Fortune telling was a popular and lucrative trade. Nearly all the clients were female, many of the servant class. Before women were allowed to join the police force undercover volunteers were employed to trap unseeing seers.

TWELVE KNOTS IN A HANDKERCHIEF

Just before Christmas in 1869 Eliza Roberts was on the knock in Frederick Street, Edgbaston. She specialised in telling fortunes to gullible housemaids. A servant, Mary Ambler, was desperate to know what the future held: would she ever be able to escape the confinement of service? Eliza instructed Mary to fetch a skirt, petticoat, a pair of boots and a chemise. Mary duly complied and handed over the garments. Another servant was persuaded to pass on her life savings of 2s. 6d.

Thus remunerated, Eliza told the girls to tie twelve knots in a handkerchief and look in a mirror. Here they would see the faces of their future husbands. To aid the charms the girls were to breathe upon a piece of tape. As the maids faithfully carried out the instructions, Eliza departed into the night, promising to return with the girls attire and cash. Needless to say the girls saw neither their future husbands nor their clothes or money again.

The Judge's predictions were more accurate than Eliza's: he said that she'd see the inside of a prison for the next six months…and she did.

THE GREAT SEER OF BIRMINGHAM

Miss Ellen Potter regularly wrote to seers and fortune-tellers whose adverts appeared in newspapers. She habitually enclosed fees, ranging from 6d. to 2s. 6d., with her requests for prophetic knowledge. Strangely no-one ever predicted that she was going to be ripped off.

In 1882 Ellen received a reply from the 'Great Seer'. Anxiously discarding the envelope, the future-junkie from Huddersfield hurriedly unfolded her communication and earnestly began reading with the same air of expectation and excitement she experienced when receiving her first forecast many years previously. Something about the wording and predictions seemed vaguely familiar. It was uncanny, the Great Seer was forecasting exactly the same path in life as had been predicted some seven years previously. Ellen, who religiously kept all her correspondence, quickly found the previous missive and began reading…

> …the course of your love will resemble that of a shallow brook which, dashing over numerous impediments, is yet thwarted by a mountain…

She glanced back at the letter she had recently received…

> …the course of your love etc. etc. etc.

The two communications were identical. The predictions were made public in Birmingham Police Court in May 1882, when John Hartwell, aka the Great

Seer, was charged with *'obtaining numerous sums of money from credulous people all over the country by false pretences'*. The 28-year-old from West Bromwich had sent the same message to hundreds of desperate domestics and gullible girls. An edited version of the mumbo jumbo is given below:

> *Wednesday will be your most noted day for good fortune, Saturday for evil; and the seventeenth day of the month will prove a great day of note in your horoscope of fate…Go westward if for gain, eastward if for honour or fame, and the whole bias of your fate turns on a certain journey at a future period of your life. There is a change approaching in your horoscope of fate; take due advantage of it. You would succeed in skillful trades or in dealing with the rich and attending to the wishes of the wealthy, also in travelling, voyaging and visiting distant lands…Cabinet print enclosed for the 2s. 6d.*

John was a wily character who anticipated trouble from the law, so with each fortune he enclosed a print, arguing that the fee mentioned was for the cheap reproduction. The predictions were free and he stood by them!

MAGISTRATE'S CLERK: *But your letter tells her that if she goes eastward she will get honour and fame…*

PRISONER: *And I am sure it will come true* (Laughter).

MAGISTRATE'S CLERK: (to witness) *Have you made up your mind whether to eastward or westward?* (Renewed laughter).

We know the way the prisoner went – downward for four months.

With women barred entry to the police force prior to WW1, amateur volunteer detectives were used to bust offenders perpetrating crimes against females. One such volunteer was Elizabeth Ashton, who visited Sara Howell at Back Rocky Lane, Hechells.

Described as a 'sallow-complexioned woman' Sara might well have had some visionary powers, for she was certainly suspicious of her visitor, informing the undercover agent that she had no desire to take on new customers, as she'd heard police were operating in the area!

As always, though, money talked and so, eventually, did Sara. Elizabeth Ashton trotted out her prearranged spiel, confiding that she suspected her husband of playing away, openly wondering what the outcome would be. Adopting the gravitas of a Mystic Meg, Sara cut a pack of playing cards and against all odds informed the distraught customer that the woman her husband was having an affair with had dark hair! A wine glass, which would magically charm back the errant husband, was then produced and a rosy future predicted. Crossing her palm with copper – 3d. – Elizabeth bid her farewell.

The couple next met in the courtroom where Sara was fined forty shillings with costs.

In December 1896, Martha and Emma Bowen were charged at Birmingham police-court with pretending to tell fortunes. During a two hour surveillance by the police from 7pm – 9pm no fewer than thirty-two women visited their house. During the raid a copy of one of the set texts for fortune-tellers 'Raphael's Book of Fate' was seized. The sisters were sent down for one month each with hard labour.

THE FEMALE BLONDIN

The daring crossing of Niagara Falls by Jean Francois Gravelet, better known as Blondin, captured the imagination of the thrill-seeking public world-wide. A string of imitators quickly followed his lead, performing high-wire walks in many major cities throughout the world.

Birmingham's answer to the dashing, death-defying Frenchman was a rather unlikely character. Aged 38 and the mother of six children, Selina Powell was expecting her seventh as she mentally prepared herself for her act in Aston Park on July 20th 1863.

A crowd of 14,000 gathered for the performance and clapped enthusiastically as Selina, showing no nerves, made two successful crossings of the tightrope pitched at a height of twenty-five feet. Not quite on a par with Niagara Falls one may argue but, unlike Selina, Blondin did not have both hands and feet chained and a sack over his head.

Maybe it was over-confidence, maybe a strong gust of wind, probably a miscalculation, but on the third crossing the thrills turned to spills. The shocked crowd gasped as one as Selina lost her balance and hurtled towards the ground. Both mother and unborn child were killed on impact.

The crowd, high on a balloon ascent, fireworks and a few bevvies, immediately sobered up. Fathers and mothers averted their children's gaze from the crumpled heap that a few seconds earlier had been a healthy artiste. They slunk home as the entertainment, like Selina's life, prematurely drew to a close.

Such is human nature, everybody started looking for someone to blame. Even Queen Victoria, who had opened the park, threw in her sixpennny worth in a letter condemning such acts. In his reply to Osborne House the Mayor of Birmingham wrote that the tragedy had occurred in Aston, which was not under his jurisdiction. He also informed the concerned monarch that a fund had been set up to help the bereaved family.

Aston Park closed the following year but there remained an insatiable demand for wacky, off-beat entertainment in the form of the freak shows very much frowned upon today. Amongst the attractions to Birmingham's Onion Fair in 1874 were 'giants, dwarves, fat women and animal monstrosities.' Enough said.

CABBAGES IN THE THEATRE

An original form of blackmail was attempted against actors and actresses in the Birmingham theatre world of the 1880s. After evening shows thespians were accosted on their way home by rogues from the gallery. If a member of the cast refused to stand a few beers for these undesirable members of their audience, the roughs would jeer and rant every time he/she spoke on stage. Not much threat for a pantomime villain perhaps, but most disconcerting for a Hamlet or Richard III.

Mr. King, who played the Emperor in Aladdin at the Prince of Wales Theatre, had been bothered for a couple of bevvies and flatly refused to part with any of his hard-earned lucre. The following evening, as he opened his mouth to utter his first lines, his lips moved but all the audience heard were loud hisses, boos and catcalls from the gallery. Every other member of the cast was listened to attentively, the barracking started only when the Emperor spoke.

The pantomime was further interrupted with the appearance of a large cabbage on stage. Thrown from the gallery the vegetable struck Aladdin (Miss Hill) full in the face. This was no comment on the ham acting – indeed if it had have been, and the tradition continued, the set of a certain motel in the area would have become a veritable vegetable stall. The flying cabbage had in fact been directed at Mr. King, who'd been standing next to Aladdin.

Let's hear some of the testimony from court in March 1880:

73. Having refused to shout drinks for gallery roughs the Emperor is catcalled every time he opens his mouth. Other players were greeted with respectful silence.

CHARLES BAKER: *I am a tube-drawer and on Saturday night was in the right-hand side of the gallery. I saw the cabbage thrown by the prisoner.*

MR GEM: *How near were you to him when he threw it?*

C. B: *About three or four yards from him.*

M. G: *Did he stand up or sit down when he threw it?*

C. B: *He stood up.*

M. G: *Then you could see him plainly?*

C. B: *Yes, sir.*

M. G: *Had you seen the cabbage before?*

C. B: *Yes; he came walking down with the cabbage in his hand.*

THE OUTRAGE AT THE PRINCE OF WALES THEATRE - BIRMINGHAM

M. G: *Did he say anything when he had it in his hand?*
C. B: *No, sir.*
M. G: *Do you know where he bought it?*
C. B: *No, all I saw was the prisoner throw it. He came up to the right-hand corner of the gallery and then threw it.*
M. G: *Did you see it strike Miss Hill?*
C. B: *Yes, sir; it was not meant for her though.*
M. G: *It was meant for someone near her, perhaps?*
C. B: *Yes.*
M. G: *How do you know it was not meant for her?*
C. B: *Because it was meant for the Emperor. They said so.*
M. G: *Who said so?*
C. B: *A good many of them.*
M. G: *Why don't they like him?*
C. B: *I don't know I am sure.*

M. G: *It is this particular Emperor they don't like and not emperors in general, is it not?* (Laughter).
C. B: *Yes, sir. Emperors are not very comfortable in many places.*
M. G: *Why did they throw it at him?*
C. B: *Because he would not give them beer or "summut".*
M. G: *It seems, then, he is an emperor who does not behave like a prince.* (Laughter).

William Mitchell, described as a rough-looking fellow, did not testify in his own defence and was sent down for two months.

Police were accused of all manner of indiscretion by those who stood in the dock. After reading reports of internal discipline, there's a good chance that many of the accusations were true.

CAN YOU READ? CAN YOU WRITE? CAN YOU FIGHT?

74. This police station, in the suburbs, was converted from homes in the late 19th century. With the rapidly increasing population more and more cells were needed to accommodate drunken offenders.

What would the life of a large town be without the much despised policeman. He 'watches our pockets' when we are sober, and if some rumours are to be believed, he reverses the action when we are unduly exilerated.

Birmingham Graphic 1883.

The Victorian police authorities had a permanent recruitment problem. Pay was poor and many men hacked the job for only a few months before resigning. Not only were they disenchanted with the financial rewards, they ran the daily risk of being attacked and spat upon – and that before they went on the beat. Internal discipline was extremely harsh. Officers were fined and fired for trivial misdemeanours. The following are typical offences from the 1850s and 60s:

Standing in a slovenly manner before the Chief Superintendent.

Sitting down asleep in a brewhouse.

Sitting upon a doorstep.

Sitting down in a shutter box.

Parading at the Public Office Yard without new uniform trousers.

Being in a brothel for five minutes when on duty and concealing himself from P.S.Gibbons.

Losing cape and taking one belonging to another constable.

Not discovering a quantity of night soil.

Absent from beat for 30 minutes. Found in a tub asleep at 2am.

Making use of highly improper language when spoken to relative to duty.

Reported sick and when visited found drunk in bed.

Assaulting P.S. and P.C.s when taken to station.

Receiving bribes (viz 1shilling and five shillings) from a licensed victualler.

Being drunk on duty and assaulting civilians.

One man's disciplinary record, chosen entirely at random, is fairly typical. Edward Henry Jones joined the force as a 22-year-old in January 1857. In his first year he was punished on seven occasions for:

> bringing an improper chart to the station (fined two day's pay, 14 days drill); gossiping in Hagley road (3 days drill), being absent from his beat and making use of insolent language to P.S.Frankish (7 days drill), losing his beat card (caution), reporting himself sick after quarrelling with and striking P.C. Bywater (fined one day's pay, 7 days drill and put on trial for 13 months); sitting down to dinner improperly dressed (caution); being absent from punishment drill (1 day's square drill).

Jones, like many of his colleagues, resented the harsh discipline and was given a further week's drill for improper conduct towards P.S. Johnson when leaving the watch committee room. He lasted a total of just four years before being dismissed for *'highly improper and disgraceful conduct towards a female.'*

In 1858 the Superintendent in Chief, R.A.Stevens – like many of his officers, seriously in debt and rather partial to a pint – sought out a novel way to curry favour with the watch committee, who'd recently become aware of his shortcomings. Stevens was in charge of security for Queen Victoria's visit to Birmingham and viewed the occasion as a chance to impress his detractors. If the visit went well, he reasoned, his job would be safe. He wanted the Queen to see the constabulary in all its glory and therefore issued the following order on June 9th, 1858:

> *The officers on duty to make out a fresh roster, marking all the finest looking men to be sent in by 9am. 10th. inst.*

All the town's handsome police were to be paraded, while the less attractive assigned other roles. This display of beautiful bobbies may have impressed little Vicky but cut no ice with the watch committee. Stevens was laid off for 'limited efficiency' nine months after the visit.

Many officers, handsome or otherwise, were not over enamoured of their uniform and resented having to display their numbers on their collars. However, mutiny was forestalled by an order (1858) which recommended that hair should be grown on the face and neck as a protection against sore throats and *afflictions of the air tubes*. With large bushy beards concealing their numbers P.C.s could take liberties, and mete out instant justice to their heart's delight, without any fear of comeback.

This problem was addressed with a further order given six years later:

> *The Chief Superintendent has noticed several constables without numbers and their great collars turned down, some even with coloured neckties on, altogether looking very untidy as if they had no officers or were not inspected. The great coat collars are to be worn turned up and the numbers on the outside.*

75. Police van c 1881.

Another order of the time, concerning police underwear, gives us some idea of the standards of hygiene in the nineteenth century:

The Chief Superintendent and surgeon strongly recommend every man to wear flannels or woollen shirts and drawers which should be changed at least once a fortnight for the sake of warmth and health, it being cheaper to be well clothed than to be on the sick list.

Many of those reporting ill were suffering from hangovers. Alcoholism was a major problem within the police force as was noted in the diary of the police missionary in 1878:

During the short time I have been here it has been painfully evident that the moral condition of the police is greatly lowered by too free indulgence in intoxicating drinks.

The diary entry concludes with the rather optimistic resolution:

I intend to inaugurate a total abstinence movement in the force.

More chance of pigs flying.

Like beleaguered teachers today, the police were under attack from all sides. Making an arrest was not simply a case of placing a heavy hand on a shoulder and uttering the celebrated words: 'you're nicked'. Criminals neither came quietly nor acknowledged 'a fair cop': they did all they could to escape, sometimes with fatal consequences.

76. In 1875, P.C. William Lines becomes the second policeman to be killed on duty in Birmingham. Arresting officers were often set upon by drunken gangs determined to release their mates. Lines was stabbed in the carotid artery. His killer, Jeremiah Corkery, was hanged and five accomplices sentenced to life imprisonment.

77. Detail of the funeral of William Lines.. It appears the coffin lid was left open.

THE NAVIGATION STREET SIX

It is unfortunately too often the case that a tragedy is needed before a problem is properly addressed. In this case, the mortal wounding of a policeman – the second such event in Birmingham – saw the increasing problem of street violence finally confronted.

Attacks on police were fairly common, but few resulted in catastrophe. Since the founding of the force three police had survived murderous attacks upon themselves and four had been crippled. The first death came in April 1872 when, three months after being attacked with a hammer in Bristol Street, P.C Thomas Hardy died of his injuries in the lunatic asylum. His assailant, Patrick Grady, was gaoled for just two months.

In 1875, P.C.William Lines, was to go into the history books for all the wrong reasons. On the morning of March 7th he was on duty in Navigation Street. This was one of the roughest areas of the city, where women would never walk alone, even at midday, as gangs were so bold they openly *garroted* (a violent, though not fatal, form of mugging) their victims in broad daylight.

On the evening of March 6th, whilst most locals were enjoying themselves at a 'free and easy' at the Bulls Head in Fordham Street, thieves gained access to a back room in the pub, only to be spotted by a young girl. She immediately raised the alarm but the 'bullet heads' managed to escape with their haul: a vest, a pair of trousers and an empty cash box.

The following morning one of the thieves, William Downes (19), like a dog returning to its vomit, went back to the pub for a drink. Spotted by the girl a second time, Downes was swiftly apprehended. The arrest, by P.C.s Fletcher and Lines, was the easiest part of the venture; getting Downes to the cells was the hard part. Word of Downes' predicament quickly spread to his fellow gang members who immediately set out to rescue him.

If the police didn't move quick enough in situations like this, they were often thwarted in their duty by abusive, stone-throwing louts, who often waded in to effect the release of their pals. Fletcher and Lines were not quick enough. Heavily outnumbered they were waylaid by a gang of screaming youths, wielding knives. Both were savagely stabbed. Lines received the most serious injury: the puncturing of his carotid artery. Over the next couple of weeks the thirty-one-year-old, racked by excruciating pain, fought bravely for his life. Dutiful to the end, and despite his immense suffering, Lines managed to provide a description of his attacker shortly before his death. He left a wife and ten-year-old daughter.

The silent majority came out in their tens of thousands to pay respect to P.C. Lines. The coffin lid bore the inscription:

**WILLIAM LINES
Died 24th March 1875**

**'When duty called him
No fear appalled him'**

Meanwhile the police made six arrests, and as the result of witness statements, eventually charged a young man of Irish descent with inflicting the fatal blow. Jeremiah Corkery was described in the press as a *'repulsive looking young fellow of the very lowest and most violent sort'*. He had received his first conviction for stabbing when only ten years old, but the five years he spent in a reformatory failed to reform him. He went back later for theft.

His murder trial saw a courtroom packed with spectators, a vast number of whom were friends and relations of Corkery and his five co-accused. With the return of a guilty verdict after just ten minutes of deliberation, the Judge took the most severe line possible, condemning Corkery to death and the other five rioters to life imprisonment, a truly draconian sentence for the times. The youths were led away screaming obscene oaths at all and sundry while, from the visitors' gallery rose the wails of the youths' female relatives and friends. Amid screams, wailings and cursing, the scene bore all the hallmarks of the harrowing of hell.

Chained together 'the Navigation Six' were bundled into a police van where they defiantly sang filthy and uproarious songs.

Once separated from their peers, gang members quickly became pathetic and weak individuals. Once Corkery had had time to reflect upon his fate, and once all appeals had failed, the young Irishman swiftly lost his false bravado. He did not sleep at all on the eve of his execution and ate little during his last two days, but he did admit his guilt – or so reporters were told – confessing: *I did it and no one else*. Other sources, however, suggest he declined the court's offer of mercy, maintaining his innocence to the end.

Corkery was led half-swooning to his place of execution in Warwick.

At his home a 'real old Irish wake' was held, the young man's corpse being represented by a pillow surrounded with candles.

Although the execution of Corkery and harsh sentences passed on his accomplices didn't stop street crime, they sent out a very strong message that assaults on the police would be severely dealt with in the courts. There were always some willing to chance their arm however.

HARD CHEESE

The sort of altercation faced almost daily by beat bobbies was played out in Coleshill Street in 1890. A 19-year-old hawker, Samuel Turner, refused to accompany P.C. Morley to the station after being arrested on a drunk and disorderly charge. Turning on the constable he began to use his shins as a football.

A fellow inebriate, 28-year-old William Henry Cheese, a hard man, was watching the match and fancied a bit of the action. He shouted out to his friend:

Are you going or not Sammy?

No, I ain't came back the reply.

Well then here goes for a _____ row, added Cheese, pulling a stone from his pocket. Not renowned for his grasp of grammar he added:

Out goes your _____ brains.

Cheese propelled the stone and in a scene reminiscent of a silent comedy it rebounded off P.C. Morley's helmet and shattered a plate glass window. A second stone was thrown but the policeman's call for assistance on his whistle was answered. Turner was sent down for two months while Cheese got three.

Physically assaulted on the streets police were also verbally insulted in the courtroom. In the early 1900s peaky blinders, mufflers round scraggy necks and cloth caps pulled down to the level of their eyebrows, would

78. *Navigation Street, 1904. When night fell one of the most dangerous areas of the city.*

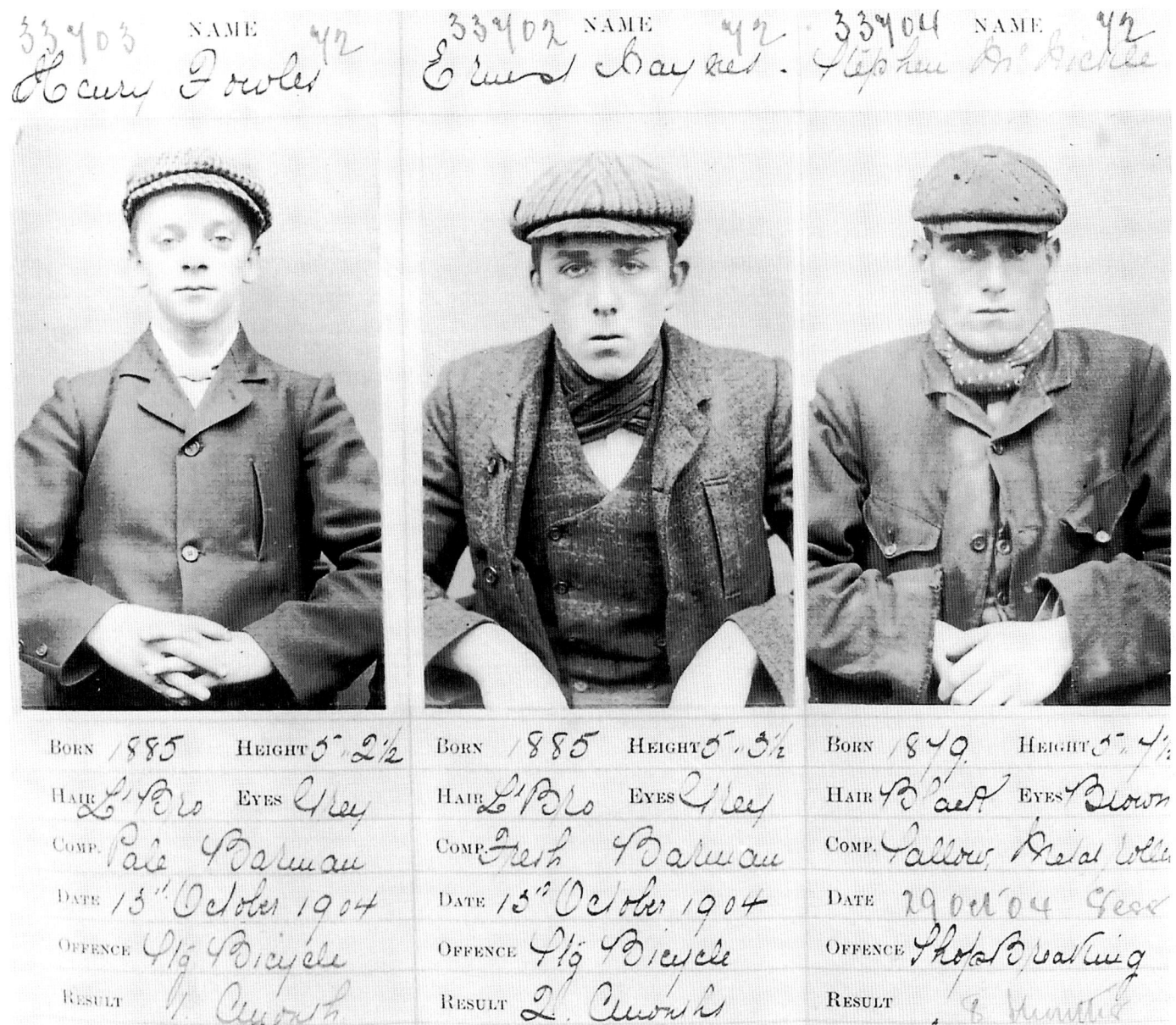

79. Three of the infamous Birmingham 'peaky blinders'. The name originated from their use of the peaks of their caps to temporarily blind their victims. Throughout the late Victorian and Edwardian periods many references were made by court reporters to men 'having the appearance of a peaky'. The foul-mouthed young men stalked the streets in drunken gangs, insulting and mugging passers-by.

Harry Fowles of 7, Coleshill Terrace and Ernest Haynes were convicted for stealing a bicycle from a well-known Birmingham cyclist, Ralph Youster. The victim left his cycle outside a factory in Henrietta Street for about four minutes. When he returned he caught a glimpse of the back of a man cycling away furiously on his bike. Despite a long exhausting pursuit he couldn't catch the thief, who was later arrested trying to sell the machine.

Stephen McNickle, from Back 66, Cuckoo Road, was charged with breaking into a draper's shop just 11 doors from his home and stealing goods to the value of £6. Every self-respecting thief knows you don't do it on your own doorstep. In mitigation he told the court he was unemployed, had a wife and two children and could not see them starving.

pack the visitor's benches. When details of attacks upon the police were related loud cries of 'Hear! Hear!' filled the court to echoes of 'Contempt'.

Police recruitment and ill-discipline remained problems into the twentieth century. Although not officially documented, the story of Chief Constable Rafter's recruitment drive in Ireland has the strong ring of truth about it.

In order to combat the high levels of crime in the Summer Lane area in 1901, the Chief Police Constable, who had several years experience in Ireland, crossed to the Emerald Isle and conducted some of the speediest interviews ever. Three simple questions were asked: Can you read? Can you write? Can you fight? If the answer to all three was 'yes' the men sailed for England.

SPARKS AT SPARKHILL

The only real check on police activities were the Watch Committees, who followed up allegations of misconduct. Their investigations were not solely confined to the lower ranks, however. In 1904, following questions raised in the House of Commons, Superintendent Pitt was dismissed for birching two teenage boys at Sparkhill. After vigorously denying the accusations he finally came clean in a letter to the local newspaper:

> I acknowledge birching both the boys although it was not done with any idea of extorting evidence. Heeks did ask to be birched, as I have already stated. With regard to Taylor, the provocation I received made me lose control of myself. When preventing him from assaulting Heeks, the boy kicked me and used vile and insulting language which caused me to lose my self-restraint. Fully realising the seriousness of what I had done and the consequences, not so much to myself as to my family, I could not bring myself to acknowledge the full facts. I very much regret implicating the other officers. No one has a greater abhorrence of a liar than myself, but I thought it would do nobody any harm, and perhaps save my wife and family from ruin...

Pitt went on to shoulder the blame entirely, attributing his conduct to stress caused by the indiscipline of his men and the high levels of crime in the area.

80. The birch and birching stall now on exhibit at the West Midlands Police Museum. This may well have been the equipment used by Superintendent Pitt which led to his dismissal.

81. Police were brought over from Ireland to deal with the lawless inhabitants of Summer Lane, home to all manner of law-breakers.

OUT OF SIGHT, OUT OF MIND?

Before the opening of the Borough Gaol offenders from Birmingham served their time in Warwick. As many prisoners were still being transported in the first half of the century there was no real demand for large penal institutions. Moor Street Police Station, built in 1806, consisted of a courtyard, two dayrooms, a kitchen and sixteen sleeping cells. Prisoners were given a pennyworth of bread and a slice of cheese twice a day and 'use of the pump'.

Once colonies refused to accept the motherland's misfits, provision had to be made for them at home. Dark, austere prisons, many of which are still in use today, were built in or near large cities. Furnished with 336 cells (increased to 612 in 1885) Winson Green opened for business in 1849.

The appointment of the first Governor of Winson Green was very controversial. Captain Alexander Maconochie was a man with ideas decades ahead of his time, who'd learnt his job in the world's most notorious penal colony. Not Devil's Island, something of a club mediteranne in comparison, but Norfolk Island, the most depraved and dangerous outpost in British prison history.

Maconochie was an exception to the rule of prison governors for the times (1840s). He was not of the normal hang 'em and flog 'em frame of mind, being more a reform 'em and praise 'em man. During his time on the Island Maconochie had the gallows dismantled, discarded the double-loaded cats used by the floggers and set up what was, for the times, a most enlightened regime. Just one act of humanity amongst many illustrates the faith the Governor had in human nature and his ability to help even the most disturbed of prisoners.

Charles Anderson was arrested for burglary and transported to Sydney. Here he was considered so uncontrollable, because of brain damage following a wound to the head, that the authorities isolated him on Goat Island, a rock in Sydney harbour. Here he spent two years, naked and tethered by a long leash. He was treated as a freak in a travelling fair and colonists would row out to his rock where they threw stale bread and offal at what they considered to be this sub-human foul-smelling savage. Sleep came with difficulty as the estimated 1,500 punishment lashes he had received had never properly healed and were periodically infested with maggots.

Eventually Anderson was transferred to the Norfolk Island regime, notoriously the harshest in the world. Here, ironically, he met with the first acts of kindness he had ever experienced in his whole life. Maconochie gave him a job, importantly away from the taunts and jibes of the other prisoners. He was put in charge of some half-wild bullocks which he managed to tame, and was congratulated, probably again for the first time in his life. Although he never fully recovered his sanity, the savage became 'civilised' and settled in his bearable existence.

Many of Maconochie's staff, however, considered their Governor too liberal and one of his subordinates expressed anxieties behind his boss's back when writing to London:

82. The appropriately named Margaret Lawless, along with her clerk accomplice, was indicted in 1897 for stealing a portmanteau with various articles from London and N.W. Railway on 8th June. Later the same month she purloined a lady's coat, vest and skirt. The 22-year-old actress, along with Walter Skelton, confessed to thirteen other robberies. Lawless, who was the dominant partner, was sent to prison for eighteen months followed by three years police supervision. Skelton served twelve months..

Captain Maconochie fancies himself supreme. [A] most radical change is wanted here immediately. The place bears no more resemblance to what a penal settlement should be than a playhouse does to a church...

Consequently, the reformer was ordered to return. In 1849, at the age of 62, thanks to the intercession of a barrister, Matthew Hill, then Recorder of Birmingham, Maconochie was appointed as the first governor of the recently-opened Winson Green prison. The years on Norfolk Island had taken their toll and the Captain's health was beginning to fail. Nonetheless he pressed on with his reforms and continued to believe in a comparatively humanitarian approach to prisoners, much to the annoyance of his sadistic deputy-governor, William Austin.

Maconochie's liberal attitudes were no better appreciated in Birmingham than on the other side of the world and, after just two years, he was replaced by the hard-line Austin. Maconochie died in obscurity in 1860 at the age of 73.

Governor Austin had spent twenty-five years at sea and served his prison apprenticeship in Tothill Fields Prison in London. Austin was an uncompromising bastard with a cruel streak. He reported for duty at 5.55 am on the dot, stood rigidly to attention saluting the centre of the prison before thoroughly inspecting the warders. The prison soon descended into a mini torture chamber with illegal punishments by warders becoming the norm. A trade instructor in the gaol gave up his job to blow the whistle on the cruelties perpetrated by the new regime. Let's hear some of his accusations:

> *Another case of cruelty is that of Charles Devall, committed 15th October last, convicted 22nd October – 18 months hard labour. Upon his entering the gaol he was threatened by an officer with 'I'll grind the soul out of you. You shall not leave this gaol alive!' The consequence was the man was disheartened, ultimately died, and a week before he died his coffin was made by the Governor's orders.*
>
> *Another case is that of Thomas Brown received in gaol on the 18th. February; crime, begging; sentenced to 14 days H.L. The Governor did with his own hands throw four pails of water upon the poor man on Saturday 28th February, one of the coldest days in the winter, and leave him in his wet clothes for two hours in an underground cell.*
>
> *Another case of cruelty is that of keeping men and boys upon the cranks without their food for days together, as I have repeatedly heard the chief warder boast of keeping them seven days together, putting them into strait jackets for thirteen hours together, strapping them to the walls from exhaustion with a high stock round their necks, nearly strangling them.*

The sadistic regime was exposed when details of the unbelievably cruel treatment of a 15-year-old boy reached the ears of the authorities in London.

When committed to the Borough Prison in March 1853, Edward Andrews stood just five feet tall and was spare of frame. He was sentenced to three months hard labour for stealing 4lbs. of beef. Having previously been found guilty of the typical juvenile offences of stealing garden fruit and throwing stones, this was Edward's third conviction. Like most of his contemporaries he could not read, had no idea of religion, and, according to the chaplain. was 'a very ignorant poor boy'.

83. Under the sadistic regime at Winson Green in the early 1850s, prisoners were expected to make 10,000 turns of the crank per day. Those who could not complete the task had their meagre rations cut and were often abused

On 30th March Edward was put to work on the crank in a separate cell in the basement of the juvenile ward. The old crank machine was placed against the wall and the labour was performed by turning the handle upon which a weight was hung. The weight was normally in proportion to the prisoner's strength: 5lbs. for juveniles; 10lbs. for adults. Prisoners were expected to perform 10,000 revolutions per day, an average of one full turn every two seconds! 2,000 revolutions were expected before breakfast, 4,000 before dinner and the remaining 4,000 before supper. Not even Tarzan could have performed such an undertaking and Edward was no Tarzan. Punishment for not completing tasks on time consisted of withholding meals and/or a diet of bread and water.

The labour was much too strenuous for the tiny Edward, who, try as he might, could not make the 10,000. He was sentenced by the chief warder to three days bread and water on three consecutive Sundays.

By 16th April the half-starved lad could no longer turn the crank. He was duly reported for being lazy and placed in a punishment jacket for 4-5 hours and collared – strapped to the wall. This particular form of punishment was greatly favoured by Lieutenant Austin.

The boy naturally grew weaker and in an act of defiance deliberately damaged his crank, and, against the rules, began to shout and scream in his cell. Two very stubborn wills were on a collision course. To Lieutenant Austin, Edward was simply defiant. As a consequence he spent all his time either on the crank, which he regularly damaged, or strapped to the wall. A bucket of water was kept in the cell lest the young man faint but was often thrown over the shivering prisoner for the guard's amusement.

However stubborn, no fifteen-year-old boy could endure such treatment indefinitely. The chaplain heard Edward *wailing most piteously and speaking of his misery and wretchedness, complaining he could not do his work because of a lack of food.*

On 19th April Edward bluntly refused to turn the crank and was once again left hanging from the wall. Further punishment was ordered due to the dirty state of his cell, so he was deprived of his bed until 10 pm.

Eight days later the boy had lost his will to live. In one final act of desperation he harnessed his remaining strength and resolve, and, balancing himself on a stool, attached a hammock strap to a bar on the window. Tying the other end round his neck he then kicked the stool away.

A Royal Commission held into the case, the findings of which are still held by Birmingham Library, insisted that Austin and Blount, the prison surgeon, stand trial at Warwick Assizes. Austin was indicted on ten counts of having practiced *various cruelties by hooks, nails, strait jackets & c upon the person of Edward Andrews, formerly a prisoner at the gaol and who committed suicide there on the night of 27th April 1853.*

Both men were found guilty and sentenced to three months' imprisonment. There is some debate as to whether they actually served their time.

A mention of some prison rules from 1866 helps illustrate the dehumanising effects of even a brief stay inside.

Convicts were not referred to by name but by number. Numbers had to be worn when prisoners left their cells and no inmate was allowed to approach within five paces of another. All male prisoners serving less than six weeks, and all those on punishment, were assigned a wooden bed – not a hammock.

If sentenced to hard labour a prisoner might be kept in solitary for up to fourteen days. Hard labour of the first class consisted of the treadwheel, short drill, crank-pump, capstan and stone-breaking. Those in the second class undertook jobs such as shoemaking, tailoring, carpentry and upholstery. Female prisoners were assigned such tasks as knitting or oakum-picking.

The diet was monotonous being made up mostly of bread, gruel, potatoes and Indian meal (maize) pudding.

In 1870 the law obliging debtors to serve prison sentences was repealed. Of the 94 prisoners now eligible to walk free from Whitecross prison, 63 left immediately and 31 asked to stay another day! A man named Bannacles, in prison 27 years for debt, literally had to be thrown out. Forced so unexpectedly to make his own personal decisions and accept responsibility for himself, the fearful Bannacles took his first cautious steps to freedom, *staring about him after his long imprisonment.*

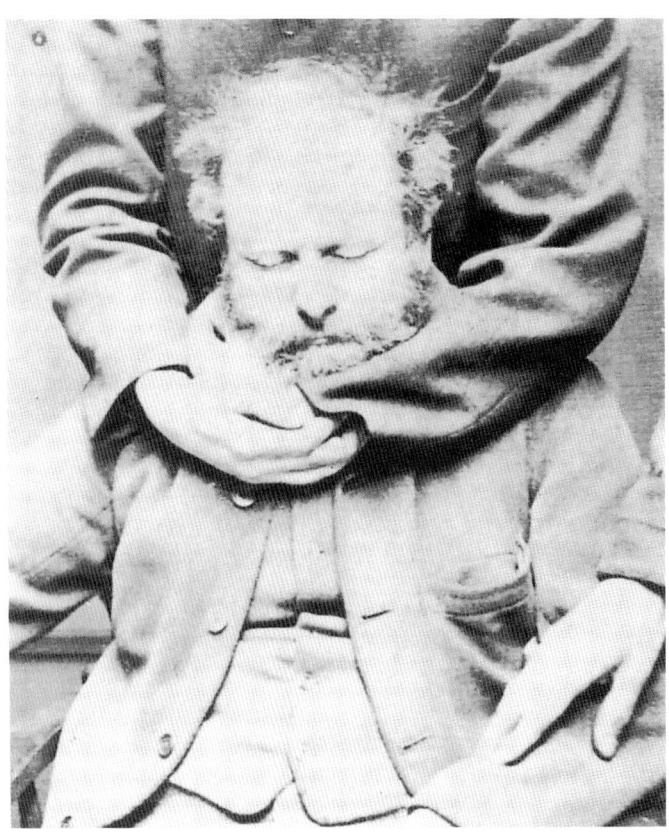

84. Henry Palmer alias Lloyd was charged in 1884 with attempting to pick pockets. He was sentenced to one month with hard labour or a fine of 40 shillings. Henry knew that sentences were much stiffer if a prisoner had 'previous' so he was understandably very reluctant to say cheese.

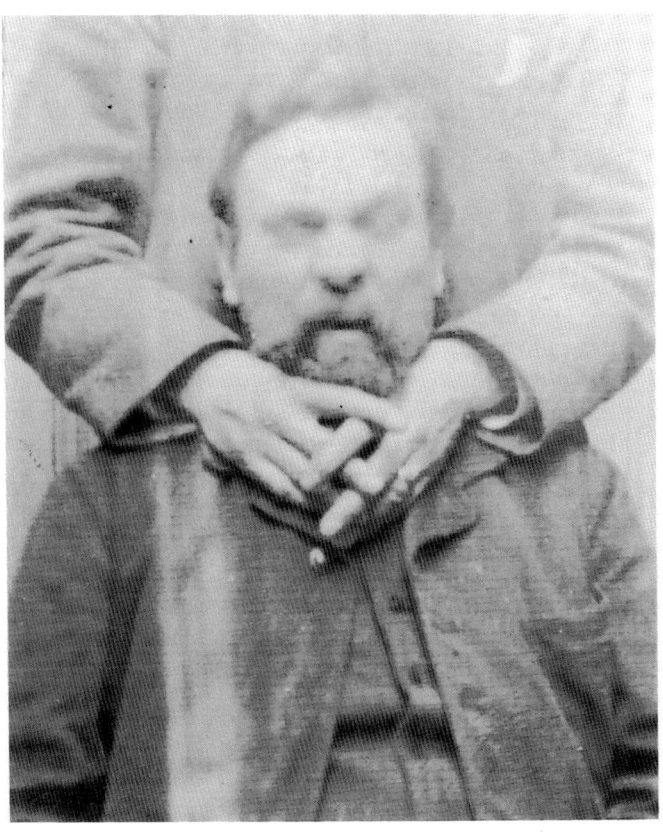

85. Another camera shy con. John Taylor alias 'Kingy Dyson' was arrested for being in possession of housebreaking implements and sent down for six weeks. A professional thief, the 55-year-old deeply resented being photographed and filed.

Whilst not impossible, escape was certainly difficult. The best way out has always been the way in. In 1882 Andrew Kenyon was sentenced to three months for attempting to pick pockets. Dressed as a 'swell mobsman' – a toff, Kenyon weaved his way in and out of shoppers at the market. He carried a cane in one hand but permanently kept the other firmly lodged in his pocket. When arrested this was discovered to be a thief's pocket, one without a bottom.

Prisoners with a trade were often made use of inside and, being a painter, Kenyon was assigned the job of painting the governor's house. One day he slipped into the premises unobserved, donned a black coat, swapped his hat for a smoking cap and appropriated a silk umbrella.

Kenyon was a cool customer. Above all else he knew that he must not rush. Sauntering through the yard he approached the prison gates, and, politely wishing the attendants 'good day', passed through unhindered.

Knowing that his absence might be discovered at any moment, he now had to act swiftly. Not far from the prison the escapee met a stranger who could further enhance his disguise. Approaching him in a feigned state of distress, Kenyon began a tall tale of his having been attacked by some roughs who, he insisted, had stolen his hat. Not wanting to go into town in a smoking cap, he offered his umbrella in exchange for the soft billycock sported by the stranger. A deal was struck and, both satisfied, the newly attired men went their separate ways.

Kenyon was finally recaptured in Wrentham Street. When asked why he had escaped, the pick-pocket, who seemed particularly proud of his exploits, replied he didn't like the food. He would have had to acquire a taste for it though, since he was charged with the theft of the governor's umbrella and clothes by the authorities, on completion of his first sentence.

86, 87. A thief, man and boy. Prison was no deterrent for Edward Hoban. His first spell inside was ten days for stealing earrings. Seven years later he had developed into a hardened criminal. In 1882, along with Samuel Martin, a fellow labourer, Edward was charged with robbing a young man from Woodcock Street.

As Joe Turner tried to make his way through a gang hanging about the streets, the loiterers parted, ostensibly to let him pass. Once in their midst Martin struck him in the mouth and Hoban made off with his watch. Both men pleaded hard for mercy and promised to change their ways. The judge was having none of it. Having read their long list of convictions he sentenced them to seven years and fifteen strokes of the cat. Hoban's last pleas in court were to his girlfriend: 'Am I done. Good bye to you. Good bye Sal.'

Kenyon need not have escaped to improve his diet. With sufficient funds practically anything could be bought from the warders who made a bee-line for well-to-do prisoners. They would drop into their cell for a little conversation during the afternoon. Prisoners were supposed to be kept ignorant of all events occurring in the outside world but one man had his *Daily Post* delivered as regularly as he did when at home.

But the prevalent problem was food, as one ex-prisoner told the same paper in 1886 *the worst part of prison, except the disgrace, is the prison fare!* His story bears repeating. Being well-off he was approached in his cell by a warder during oakum-picking and asked whether he would like to write to his wife. The letter was duly delivered with the warder receiving £1 from the Mrs for 'his troubles'. Life began to change for the better as he gratefully received:

88. In Victorian times sexual relations between men were considered as one of the most heinous of crimes and extremely stiff sentences were passed for acts that have now been decriminalised. As may be seen from the 1885 police record, 18-year-old Alfred Holmes was sentenced to spend the rest of his life in gaol.

Plenty of apples and that sort of thing. I had turkey for my Christmas dinner. I sent Christmas cards to all my children. I used to have a newspaper now and then. What I got most often was a tit-bit for my breakfast. It usually took the shape of some ham or tongue or some sandwiches as for obvious reasons the warders never brought anything that would leave bones or other traces behind it.

You see the breakfast was the easiest for them. While the cells were being cleaned out between seven and eight in the morning the doors were open so that prisoners could carry out the slops, and the warder used to step into my cell as if to see that it was alright and put the food into the pocket of my jacket.

Those without funds had to make do with grotty gruel. Meanwhile the lives of their wives outside were equally as harsh. Forced onto the job market, prison widows would do such jobs as mending chairs, sorting out rags or binding faggots, in stuffy rooms with urchins crawling about. They often did not know nor care why their husbands were doing bird. *He's doin' three months for pinchin' summat* would be a common reply when asked about the absence of their men.

Some women had no intention of wasting their time waiting for husbands/boyfriends. The Chief Warder of Winson Green remembers finding a book in which a prisoner named Jones penned a sentence after his sentence:

Good-bye Lucy dear
I'm parted from you for seven long year – Alfred Jones.

A cynical prisoner who picked up the same book a short time later added:

If Lucy dear is like most gals
She'll give you few sighs or moans
But soon she'll find among your pals
Another Alfred Jones

89. 24-year-old soldier Harry Wood was sentenced to five years for the same offence. No details of either case were reported in the local press.

90. Christine Bradshaw was charged with stealing a bucket and coal-hod from an out-house at the back of the Roebuck in Moor Street. Like many offenders when questioned in court she contradicted herself. After initially saying she was a widow, Christine then pleaded for mercy on the grounds that she had a husband who was at the point of death. The judge would have none of it and sent her down for three months in 1871.

91. Margaret Neary spent Christmas 1871 in prison for stealing a shirt valued at 3s. 6d. from the shop-door of Samuel Timmins, draper of 2, Stafford Street. Not the most subtle of thieves, Margaret simply unfastened the shirt from the place where it was fixed, concealed it under her apron and made off down the street. Three months.

92, 93. Mary Ann Smith (21) and Elizabeth Harris (18) and a male accomplice worked as a team. On 15th November 1870 a man walking down Digbeth was grabbed and pinioned from behind while the two girls rifled his pockets, stealing a handkerchief. Both prisoners, able to read and write imperfectly, were known to the police. Mary Ann had been convicted seven times in the previous eighteen months, mostly for assault. Elizabeth, from Freeman Street, was rather conservatively described in the newspaper as 'bearing by no means a favourable character'. Both were sent down for three months. Their male accomplice was never found

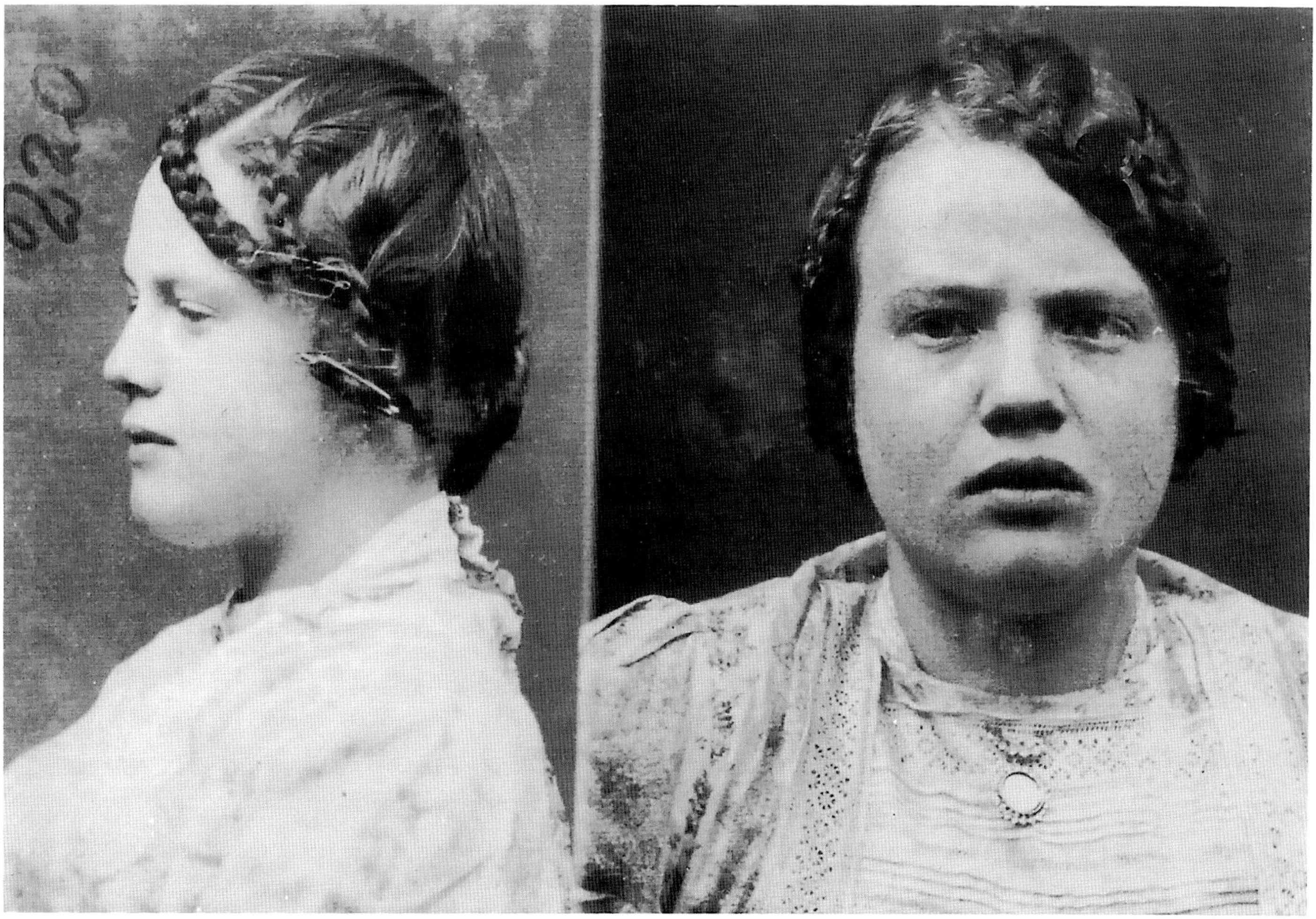

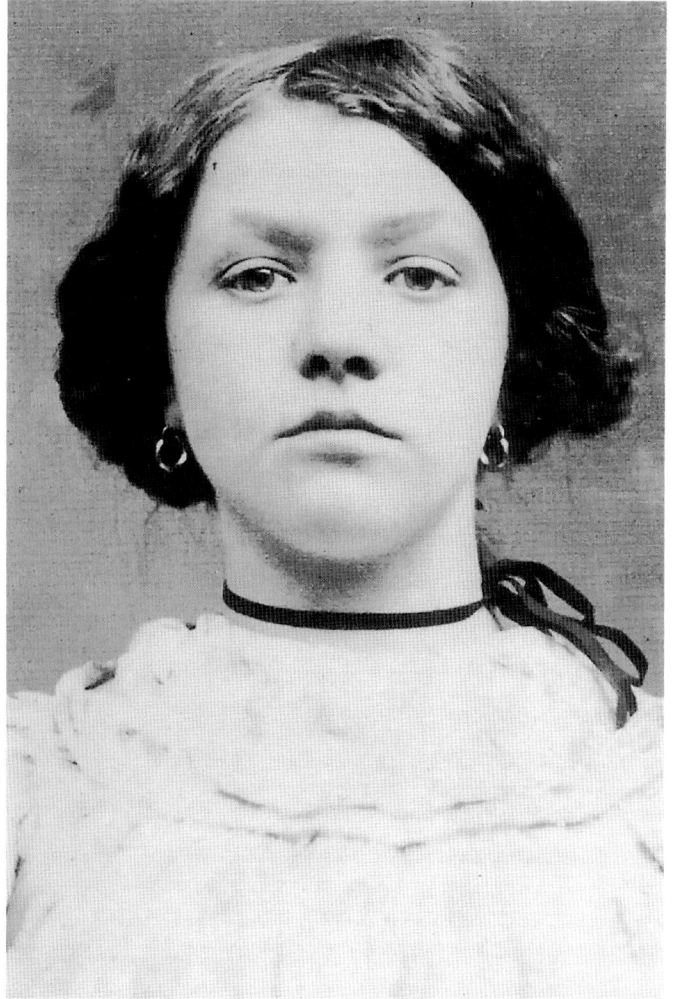

94. Amy Gill (above), 20, from Bordesley Street, Ellen Pickering, 20, from Lancaster Street and Leah Jenks, 19, from Moseley Street, brass polishers all, were charged together in 1906 with stealing laces from No. 1 Bull Ring and assaulting Florence Kirkman, the wife of the owner.

At 5pm on a Monday the three removed laces from a box just outside. When the shopkeeper asked for payment or return, Pickering suddenly struck Florence violently in the face and all three set about her. The victim later testified that it seemed they all went mad. They dragged her about, pulled her hair and the more she asked them to desist the worse they got. They pulled two good handfuls of hair from her head and her shoulder was seriously injured. Florence sought help from a nearby shop whose staff later testified that the girls used the most vile language they had ever heard in their lives.

Amy Gill, who had the words 'TRUE LOVE' tattooed on her arm, shrieking loudly, threatened the prosecutrix as she was taken down to begin her two month sentence.

95. Leah Jinks (left) escaped with the remarkably lenient fine of ten shillings for her part in the affray.

96. 17-year-old Edith Rose appeared to take a pride in her appearance. She liked the clothes but not the bills so didn't bother paying for her finery. Tattoos of BSFL on left hand and CHDFC on left forearm, meaning what?

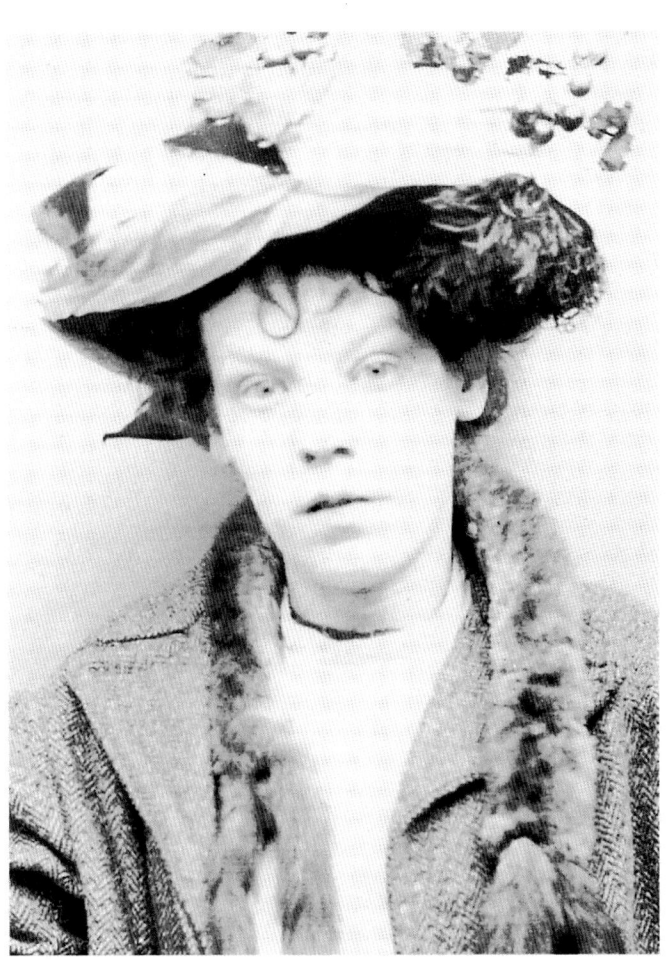

97. Annie Mitchell, another woman who had a predilection for clothes she could not afford. Six months for stealing boots - 1904. She took Tom Kelly to prison, tattooed on her arm.

98. Mary Elizabeth Durell presented herself in her best attire in court in 1896. It certainly did her no harm as she was found 'not guilty' on a false pretences charge.

99. Police files record a prisoner's complexion before their profession, hence Maggie Lines being described as 'fresh barmaid'. Maggie was found 'not guilty' on a charge of stealing a purse (1910). Another interesting photo for followers of fashion.

100, 101. Partners in crime. Clare Ashford (17) and Winifred Cooney (19). Clare graduated from short sentences for obscene language and drunken/riotous behaviour to stealing a cheese (with Winifred) from a shop door in Hockley Hill. Both were sent down for six months.

By the age of 19, Winifred was already a hardened criminal with scars and a broken nose to testify that she gave as good as she got. The spoon and fork polisher from Thomas Street was fond of her food. Apart from the cheese she stole with Clare, Winnie served three months for stealing bacon valued at 6s. 8d. Stopped by P.C. Hill in Bagot Street because she appeared to be secreting something under her aprons, Winnie and her 16-year-old accomplice argued that they had been innocently wandering along the street when two young men ran past and plopped the pieces of pig in their pinnies! Even Winifred realised the story wouldn't wash, pleading 'guilty' in court.

102. Elizabeth Henley and her male accomplice robbed John Parton of 7s. 6d. with personal violence in 1870. The sentence of 18 months seems particularly harsh but judges were determined to make an example of what we now call 'muggers'.

103. Annie Preston, a polisher acquitted on a charge of stealing a candlestick. Of more interest is the hairstyle against which there is no record of a charge.

104. Sarah Ann Birch and curlers. Another photo certain to interest the followers of fashion. There's a good chance that most of the clothes she is wearing were stolen as this was her speciality. Quite why she was photographed in front of a heavy door is unclear.

105. Mary Ann Turner, aged 19, was first arrested at 13 for being drunk and riotous. Eight more convictions for the same offence followed before the young woman from Moor Street was sent to prison for eight months for stealing a handkerchief. Mary had no intention of changing her ways. In June, 1874 entering a shoe shop with a male and female accomplice, she slipped a pair of boots to the man who made off with them. The hapless Mary was caught by the shopkeeper and sent down for fifteen months followed by two years' police supervision.

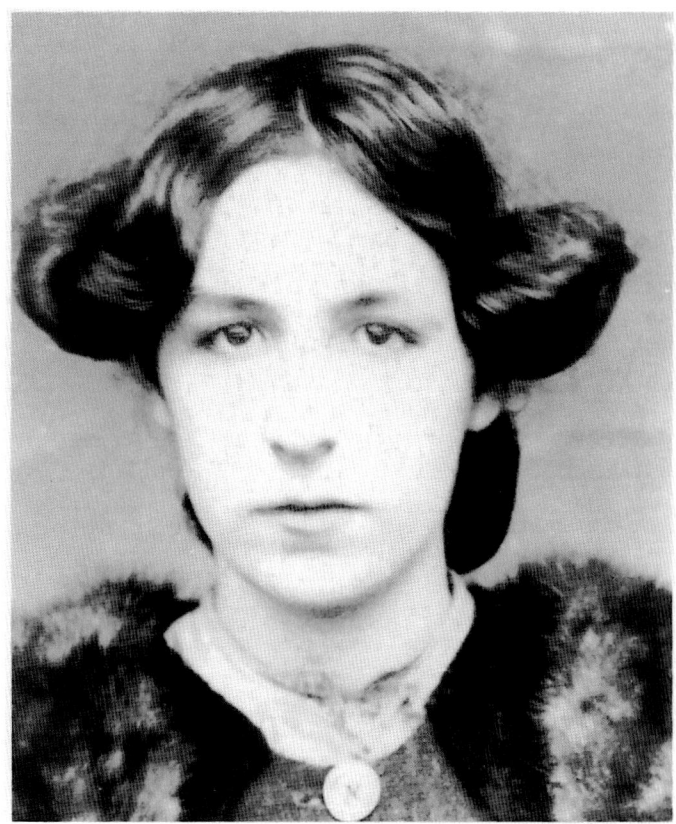

106. Mary Ann Gallagher, (top left) a penmaker, was charged with violently assaulting Stephen Kerrigan and robbing him of his hat and eleven shillings. The victim from West Brom met the 18-year-old Mary on the street. The couple repaired to a pub in Lichfield Street where he 'stood treat'. As they left Mary showed her appreciation by throwing her shawl over his head and holding him tightly whilst three male accomplices robbed him. Kerrigan managed to struggle free and soon reversed the role, holding Mary until a policeman arrived. Found guilty of robbery with violence Mary was sent down for eighteen months.

107. In 1908 John Preston, a 21-year-old cycle finisher and Kate Burke (above) a 22-year-old flower seller were charged with breaking and entering the home of Robert Walton and stealing a bangle, one crown piece and a watch chain.

The previous Thursday the pair were found not guilty of breaking into another home. The victim, Robert Walton, lived at 194, Mansell Road, Small Heath. He left his home at 7pm and returned one hour later with that horrible sinking feeling, so many of us know these days. When he tried to open the door and found it bolted from the inside he knew his house had been ransacked.

Witnesses told the police that they saw Kate Burke walking up and down the road allegedly acting as a lookout. She was joined by a male and both ran off when the police arrived. Kate later told police that she had been walking on some waste land when she saw a man run past her. Her accomplice, Preston insisted that he'd been in bed with a cold. There was not enough evidence to convict and when the 'not guilty' verdict was returned it was greeted with loud applause in the gallery.

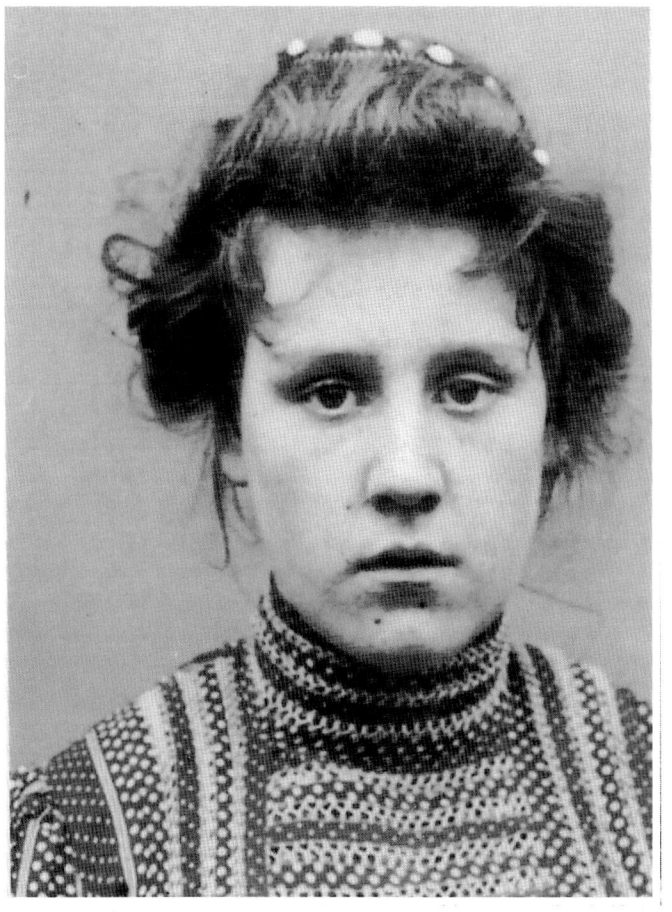

108. Elizabeth Hicks (left), a 16-year-old domestic servant convicted of stealing £10, the equivalent of about six months of her salary. Sentence: three months.

109. Three offenders, probably of more interest to followers of fashion than those of crime. The women obviously took a pride in their appearance and were better rigged out than most of their contemporaries in the mid 1890s. Perhaps crime did pay?

110. In June 1885 Edward Milford was described in the local press as a 'disgraceful fellow'. He refused to say anything in court after being charged with exhibiting obscene pictures to two little girls in Edgbaston. The prisoner accosted the children and asked them whether they had dropped a small book which he then produced. When opened the book contained a number of 'disgusting prints'. The girls told their mother and Milford was arrested near Cathorpe Park. Books and other prints were found on his person Sentencing him to three months Mr Kynnersley expressed regret that the law did not allow him to order a flogging.

111. Annie Simmonds (page 83) alias Marie Holloway. The 22-year-old made her living from thieving and prostitution. Annie, well-scarred and with three missing teeth from her upper jaw, was not averse to mixing it. A two week term for assault was followed by six months in 1875 for larceny from the person. This usually meant pickpocketing. Annie was chased and caught after stealing a purse containing 10s. 3d. from Susan Pipkin.

THE LOVER, IN THE KITCHEN WITH THE REVOLVER

Before the opening of the Assizes in 1884, Birmingham's condemned were dispatched at Warwick. From 1885 to the start of the Great War, though, eleven men were hanged in the city.

Most of the murders were domestic. Six of the eleven killers were executed for the murder of their wives/girlfriends. Two of the remaining killed men in drunken brawls. One shot a woman who was trying to defend her girl friend and another a young baby. Only one killed someone they did not know, a frail ten-year-old girl butchered in a vicious sexual attack.

Many more people were unlawfully killed but charges were often reduced to manslaughter or the perpetrator deemed insane. Most of the victims were women and the favoured methods of dispatch, revolvers and cut-throat razors.

In many ways detection was a simpler task in Victorian Birmingham. Find the body, find the boyfriend. If Cluedo had been set in Victorian times the murder bag would almost inevitably reveal the crime to have been committed in the kitchen, with the revolver, by the (jilted) lover. Let's begin our look back at the crimes of the times with two typical murders committed before the opening of the Assizes.

OH DON'T! DON'T!

Upon hearing the sighs of pleasure and squeals of delight usually indicative of a romp, Hannah White, the maid of a wealthy jeweller, couldn't resist a quick peek through the keyhole. Knowing her master to be away, she wanted to see the new household member!

There lay her mistress, 25-year-old Sarah Alice Vernon, in a passionate embrace with John Ralph, a married man. The affair was tempestuous, the couple apparently finding with each other the sexual chemistry missing from their marriages.

Hannah kept quiet…until the inquest.

A few weeks later Sarah Vernon and John Ralph boldly started stepping out in public. This was a mistake, as most of the passion of the affair depended on in its secrecy. In time the inevitable happened: the spark died. According to Ralph, he intended to give Alice the boot. According to eavesdroppers at the Welcome public house, it was Alice Vernon who gave Ralph his marching orders.

At all events, tragedy loomed. One Friday in June 1879, at 11.30pm a cabman caught a glimpse of Mrs. Vernon with a man at the canal bridge. A local heard the loud piercing screams followed by a woman's voice pleading 'Oh, don't! don't!'

Three hours later Ralph surrendered to a policeman and asked to be handcuffed. He told the startled officer that he had thrown 'Old Page's daughter Alice' into the canal.

At his trial Ralph did not deny that he had pushed his lover in and when she tried to get out had forced her back. He denied cutting the woman's throat.

Ralph's wife, despite his philandering, forgave her husband and wept bitterly at his execution at Warwick on August 26th, 1879.

112. In June 1879, John Ralph pushed his lover, Alice Vernon, into the canal. As was fairly common for the times, Ralph gave himself up to a policeman. He was hanged at Warwick some two months later.

AXED JUST ONE WEEK AFTER MARRIAGE

If a week is a long time in politics it was a whole lifetime in marriage. This was particularly so for the newly-wed Mrs. Clarke. As she bent down to tend home fires in Garrison Lane, just a week after the wedding, she was savagely axed from behind by her 32-year-old husband, Thomas.

That Clarke committed the murder in November 1883 there is no doubt; whether he was responsible for his actions was another matter. As he stood in court, his eyes permanently fixed on the ground, he heard his defence team plead for his life on the grounds of diminished responsibility. They seemed to have quite a good case, their best exhibit being the defendant himself. When asked for his plea Clarke replied:

> – Well Sir, I don't know what to say for it. I was willing to die for her, bless her. Whatever I done I can't say.
> – Then you had better plead guilty advised the judge.
> – Well then I will say I am not guilty was the defiant reply.

The defence outlined their case:

> I intend to call witnesses to show that Clarke is insane. On one occasion he cut his own throat, was taken to hospital, had it stitched up, and then, discharged a few hours afterwards, he tried to cut the stitching.

114. The 32-year-old, literally a 'mad axeman', was ordered to be detained as a criminal lunatic in the Borough Lunatic Asylum at Her Majesty's pleasure.

> He would go around the country lanes looking for wasps nests, upon finding them, he would, despite being severely stung about his hands and face, put handfuls of wasps in his pocket, only to throw them away when he got home.
> A few days ago he said at eight o'clock in the morning, 'Good morning' to a friend. The friend replied 'Good morning'. Clarke retorted, 'What do you mean saying "Good morning" at this time of night.

There is little doubt that Clarke was insane and he was sentenced to be detained at Her Majesty's pleasure in the Borough Asylum.

As we shall see, there must be severe doubts as to the sanity of other, less fortunate men *sent up the ladder to rest.*

WITH OR WITHOUT YOU

The first hanging in Birmingham for eighty years took place on March 17th 1885.

53-year-old Henry Kimberley could not live neither with nor without his lover. Finally, following seventeen years of falling out and making up, the couple agreed to split. Harriet Stewart was the instigator of the separation and she was adamant that it would be permanent. She swore, in more ways than one, that she would not live with him again. As far as she was concerned, Kimberley was history. Unfortunately he became so for all the wrong reasons.

Kimberley immediately regretted the separation. The fact that he'd received £20 and a piano whilst his former partner kept the home was of little importance. He wanted Harriet, body and soul, and if he couldn't have her…

Harriet Stewart's best friend was Mrs. Palmer, the wife of the landlord of the White Hart on Paradise Street. Two days after Christmas the pair popped into the snug of the aforementioned pub for a chinwag and a little Christmas spirit. Their conversation was rudely interrupted by the arrival of the turkey.

Henry Kimberley, at his wits end, his loneliness keenly accentuated over the festive period, pleaded with Harriet for a reconciliation. The answer was a forceful 'No!' Thereupon, the spurned man produced a revolver from his pocket and shot Harriet at point blank range. Mrs. Palmer, loyal and brave as she was, tried to defend her friend, only to be shot herself. The bullet hit home, passing through her chest, coming to rest in the lung. She fell dead to the floor.

Overpowered by the barman and customers, Kimberley ironically went to the gallows for the murder of a woman he barely knew. Harriet Stewart later recovered.

'I'LL SWING FOR YOU'

Lodgers were an economic necessity for many families with high rents and low wages. Consequently, if a marriage was not working too well, as was often the case in such trying conditions, the wife didn't have to play away. A substitute could be called on at any time. Bed and breakfast had extra depth in many households.

In the 1880s a young train driver, Harry Benjamin Jones, moved in with the Harris family at 29, Meriden Place, Sutherland Street. George Harris, a carpenter in his early thirties, had an attractive wife and children. Jones soon became besotted with his landlady and thus began a passionate affair, which lasted throughout the five years he lodged in the Harris household. He even followed the family down to Gloucester where they moved to escape his attentions. It was here that, in a fit of pique at rejection, he fired a revolver at the love in his life. She was not seriously injured but Jones spent three months in prison.

George Harris was meanwhile offered a job in Wales but his wife couldn't settle and returned with her then

115. Henry Kimberley, the first man to be hanged in Birmingham for 80 years.

four children and set up home with the man who had shot her, Harry Jones. Although this appears a case of 'the devil you know' it may have been more complicated, for the train driver asserted parental rights over the two younger children. The family lived on Jones's salary and the £1 a week sent by Mr Harris from Wales. But absence made the heart grow fonder and Mrs. Harris soon discovered that she still loved her husband.

When the carpenter returned permanently from Wales the hot-headed Jones left the house, experiencing a very keen sense of rejection. The only woman in his life, the alleged mother of two of his children, had rejected him. Her reason, she told him, was because of his bad

JONES MURDEROUSLY ATTACKS MRS HARRIS

language, but he knew better than that. The woman was a heartless whore who had duped him and dumped him for an older man. She deserved everything she got. He was inconsolable and later stormed round to the house where he shouted out:

I've shot you once and I'll shoot you again!

He was a man of his word. Jones had little trouble acquiring an old-fashioned pin-fire six chamber revolver and twenty cartridges. On 15th June 1888 he returned to Meriden Place on the pretext of demanding the return of his box of clothes. Determined to right wrongs, Jones left this letter at his digs:

I am prepared to die and I hope to meet my dear mother in heaven. I have been misled by a married woman. She swore she would never have anything more to do with Dick.
May the Lord have mercy on my soul.

With the fixated Jones skulking in the shadows, Mrs. Harris ventured out at 11.30am to draw water from a communal tap. Silently approaching from behind Jones, who had consumed several glasses of beer, took a hefty kick at the bucket, sending the water flying. The badly shaken Mrs. Harris scurried back to the safety of her kitchen. Some fifteen minutes later, believing the coast to be clear, the harassed woman made a second attempt to fetch water. Jones had now steeled himself for his course of action and, steadying his arm, took aim at the woman he once loved. The bullet buried itself high in the mother's right shoulder. Alerted by the sound of gun and groan, Mr. Harris sprinted into the yard and he too was shot, a bullet grazing his left shoulder. He turned and darted into the kitchen, securing the door, leaving his wife outside to meet her fate.

Having witnessed the mayhem he had wreaked with just two shots, Jones was determined to take as many lives as possible before shooting himself. With the force of a demon with no concern for his own safety, Jones used himself as a battering ram and charged the kitchen door, breaking the window with a single blow. He fired two more shots at the petrified Harris before climbing into the room. Harris raced off into the street via the front door in order to fetch help. He abandoned a little girl playing with her shoes by the table. The tot, one of those Jones claimed as his own, seemed unconcerned by the bluster and continued in her own little world.

When she looked up Jones cold-bloodedly shot her in the forehead.

Arrogantly, the master of all he surveyed, Jones strode casually back into the yard to finish off the child's mother. Mrs. Harris, conscious and standing, pleaded with a neighbour to rescue the surviving children:

Go and look after my little children for God's dear sake. He's killed my two babies.

Jones calmly took aim and squeezed the trigger. The last cartridge almost blasted the woman off her feet as it entered the left shoulder blade. She reeled but still stood defiantly, blood streaming down her clothes as Jones screamed:

I can't finish him but I'll finish you.

The frenzied gunman dealt two heavy blows with the butt to the brave mother's face, he then turned to the house, where he found a sleeping baby of four months. As indifferently as if he were clubbing a seal, the deranged gunman struck the defenceless child twice on the head with the butt of his gun and then reloaded.

Shouting out *'I'll swing for you'* Jones began shooting indiscriminately into the courtyard, shattering a flower pot next to one of the neighbours. By now a large crowd had assembled and Jones was soon overpowered and disarmed. For him the war was over:

You can send for the police. I've done it and I'm not going to run away.

Later, Jones said that he'd fully intended to commit suicide but the crowd had arrived too quickly. He enquired if the victims were dead and before anyone could answer, added:

I hope the _____ are. I'm happy now.

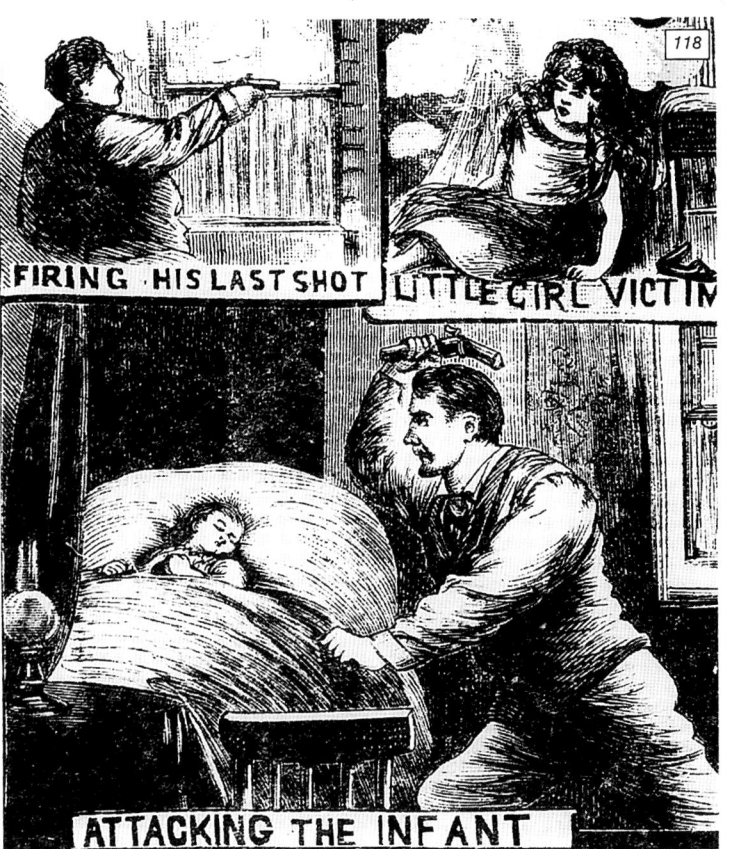

When told that little Florrie had died from a bullet to the brain, while the baby was in a serious condition, Jones expressed no remorse and wished the others had curled up their toes. At his trial at the Warwick Assizes, Henry Benjamin Jones was sentenced to death for the murder of Florrie.

Jones was the main attraction at a double execution. Nathaniel Daniels played the supporting role. Daniels showed his love for his girlfriend Emma Hastings by kissing her goodnight at the Golden Elephant Inn on Castle Street and immediately pumping two bullets into her head and chest. Daniels died instantly and was forgotten just as quickly.

As for Jones? Forever hanging around in life he did the same at the end of a rope. His neck unbroken he slowly strangled to death. Three days later one Jack the Ripper started to hog the headlines.

'CHOPPER' HARRIS

William Harris, no relation to George, had a very short fuse. His failure to control his temper was one of the main reasons he had spent a great deal of his adult life in gaol. Quite what 17-year-old Florrie Clifford saw in him we'll never know. It was certainly the worst decision of her short life when she agreed to move in with the man from William Street, Aston. Florrie set up home with Harris and his mother but when she looked like becoming a mother herself, he beat her up and Florrie went home to her mum.

When the two Cliffords called to pick up the young girl's clothing, Harris saw red and, wielding an axe, mercilessly smashed his ex about the head, completely severing her left ear. Harris threw the axe at Mrs Clifford as he fled the scene of carnage. Poor Florrie died an agonising death five days later.

Some weeks hence, Harris surrendered himself to Northampton police. There must have been doubts as to his sanity when, on receiving sentence of death, Harris turned to the court and declared:

I wish I could have got her mother as well. I would have chopped her into mincemeat and made sausages of her, and then I should have been satisfied.

For his own safety he was placed in a padded cell.

He was executed at Warwick as the crime had been committed in Aston, not then a part of Birmingham, in January 1894. Harris appeared fixated with food to the very end, shouting out to attendant reporters:

They've gave me nothing to eat, no breakfast nor nothing.

SLAUGHTER IN VYSE STREET

Crimes which most outrage the public are those perpetrated by adults on children. Parents today are ever-vigilant, hankering after the old days when children could play freely without fear of abduction and murder. But did these days really exist? Certainly not in Victorian times when many children simply disappeared never to be seen again. Many attacks and rapes were never reported being hushed up with a little blood money.

One of the cases that did come to trial was the brutal rape and murder of May Lewis in 1896, which sent shock waves through the close-knit community of Birmingham's Jewellery quarter. The details of the crime are still distressing over one hundred years later.

The blood-soaked corpse of the frail ten-year-old was discovered early one morning in a garden in Vyse Street. The police believed that it had been hurriedly abandoned, possibly because someone carrying it to the nearby canal had panicked. The house was occupied by 60-year-old messenger John Taylor and his wife. When police started questioning them about the remains found in their garden they noticed blood on the doorstep. A full scale search of the house was consequently ordered. Attempts had been made to wipe out bloodstains in several rooms and a piece of heavily stained rag was discovered in a water tank. Blood and pieces of hair were also found on a brick. John Taylor and his wife were immediately taken into custody, where they were joined three hours later by their son, Frank. The saturated 23-year-old had surrendered himself to Dudley Road police station, after what police suspected was an unsuccessful attempt to drown himself.

Even Frank Taylor's parents described him as 'a loafing good-for-nothing fellow'. The unemployed carter had been staying in a lodging house in Rea Street but still had access to his parent's home and sometimes went there when they were out. Police were convinced that all three Taylors were involved in May's death.

The trio appeared in court in a preliminary hearing the following day. Frank Taylor was described as 'a tall angular young man with a slight moustache'. He was dressed in a black somewhat threadbare suit. His mother, who stood on his left, was dressed in deep black and could not control her tears. His father appeared 'nervous and apprehensive'. Mrs. Taylor was released on bail but the two men remanded. Most of the case against the three was based on a statement provided by their daughter.

Seventeen-year-old Lizzie Taylor alleged that between 9 and 11pm. on the night of the murder 'a good deal of whispering took place' between her parents. She was told that another brother, who usually slept alone in the attic, would have to share her bed that night. It appears from this, that the original intention had been to temporarily secrete May's body in the attic. From the bloody evidence of the water tank, which was in the attic, police believed there had been an attempt to hide the body in it but it would not fit. The corpse had then been dumped in the garden and an amateurish attempt at cleaning up the bloodstains put into effect.

But who had murdered poor May and why?

Although nobody ever confessed to the murder, the police version, which seems highly likely, was as follows. On the afternoon of 10th March 1896 Frank Taylor started drinking earlier than usual in St Matthises Tavern. Mid-afternoon he went to his parent's home, spotting young May as she passed the Taylor's house on her way home from school. Quite how he enticed the poor object of his lust into his parent's home is uncertain – perhaps a promise of sweets, or an invitation to see his puppy – at all events May, in her innocence, would have followed unquestioningly.

The attack, which took place in the bedroom, was one of the most violent and cowardly assaults ever inflicted on a child in the city. At the later inquest medical evidence showed that little May had been raped 'with extraordinary violence' and her head had been so battered that the skull was smashed in several places. In his report, Dr. Burton, who carried out the autopsy, listed 'five shocking wounds on the left side of the face.'

Following the murder Frank had fallen into a drunken sleep until his parents came home. After the initial shock of finding their house smeared in blood and the pathetic body of a 10-year-old in the bedroom, they tried to protect their oaf of a son by hiding the corpse and cleaning up the house. In the meantime the murderer had fled into the night and the next they saw of him was the following day after his dip in the canal.

The cruel slaying horrified the whole population of the city and over 50,000 turned out to witness May Lewis's funeral at Witton cemetery. With only forty police on duty, control was soon lost as the masses swarmed the hearse, trampling flowers and gravestones as they went. May's tiny coffin was borne by six girls from her school, Summer Lane. Wreaths were piled waist high and hundreds and hundreds of women and girls dropped flowers into the grave.

The murder trial against Frank Taylor began on August 1st. No females were permitted to enter the courtroom. Charges against the parents had earlier been dropped, though the judge expressed his doubts, stating on record that he believed the parents were not telling the whole truth. The defence's only defence hinged on the disgraceful suggestion that it was unlikely that any young man would waylay such a dirty, underfed girl in order to rape her!

The jury took just ten minutes to find the defendant guilty of murder.

On remand, prior to his trial, Taylor had kicked anything movable and then started on the walls. Haunted by nightmares, he would regularly jump out of bed and hammer on the cell door. Following his conviction he became a lot calmer and was given fowl, mutton and a large bottle of beer for his lunch.

On 17th August 1896, the eve of execution, the prisoner went to bed at 11.30pm. He rose at 6am the following day, ate the traditional hearty breakfast and walked unassisted to the gallows. He made no confession.

When the black flag rose, a crowd of four thousand people, gathered outside the prison, burst into spontaneous applause.

119. The sensationalist reporting of Victorian Birmingham's most disgraceful murder.

LIKE A SOLDIER FALL

The following is a recipe for a traditional Victorian and Edwardian domestic murder:

One woman. One man (drunk). One cut-throat razor. One ounce of rejection. One pound of retaliation. A pinch of suicide. Stew for a month. Hang for half an hour. Serve with no remorse.

The job of defence lawyers in domestics was almost impossible. Accused murderers were either arrested at the scene of their crimes, soaked in their victims' blood or they'd owned up to their crimes, usually after an attempt on their own lives. Faced with such damning evidence, the only possible defence was to have murder charges reduced to manslaughter on grounds of diminished responsibility.

A widely held belief was that if you spent too long in the tropics the sun's rays literally went to your head, stewing the brain and causing temporary insanity. Soldiers were frequent victims.

In the winter of 1904 William Dyer's lawyer was contemplating just such a plea. Dyer was a tall man for the times, a little shy of six foot. His thin face was bronzed following a two-year stint with the 1st Warwickshires in India. He had the erect gait of the serviceman and his dark hair was neatly brushed and moustache tidily clipped. Pride in his physical appearance had been firmly drilled into him.

Dyer was discharged in December 1903. His £20 payout was largely spent on ale, his own and that of 23-year-old Patty Simpson. She was described by the *Weekly Mercury* as *a plump unfortunate*, though *Viz* would put it another way! Patty was the kind of girl who got going when the ale got flowing. As long as Dyer had the money Patty was willing and the pair, who met at Christmas, 1903, were still together two months into the new year. For many women, prostitution was a part-time occupation. When girls found compatible punters they might give up the night job and live with them, on and off, as long as funds lasted.

The 25-year-old William Dyer's artillery training was of little use to him in civvy street. After forsaking the heat and prestige of life as a soldier in India, he spent two months tramping the damp streets of Birmingham. Nonetheless he seemed happy. He had Patty, a room at No 21 Inge Street, and, if the house was overcrowded and damp, it was home and there was no shortage of beer-houses within spitting distance.

On the evening of the 3rd February 1904 William and Patty invited two friends, John and Maggie Morgan to dine with them before going on to one of the public-houses in Old Meeting Street. William and Patty made their way home at 11.15pm.

Some fifteen minutes later the ex-serviceman rushed back into the pub. He was in a distressed state with, as a witness later testified, *'waistcoat undone, his clothes disarranged and blood on his hands'*. Dyer implored Margaret Morgan to help him:

– Oh Mag, go and save her. I have done it!
– Done what?
– Done her in.

As Dyer sat in the pub in a state of shock, his tanned face having turned a whiter shade of pale, the married couple rushed to the pokey residence in Inge Street. Patty's blood-soaked limp and lifeless body was stretched without design over a cheap chair. Her throat had been savagely slashed from ear to ear. A blood-stained razor lay on the table nearby. Margaret Morgan bluntly described the scene of devastation in court:

There was a great hole in her throat and blood was running down her dress front. It was an awful sight.

With the arrival in the pub of the local police-sergeant, Dyer was questioned. He made no effort to deny responsibility:

I have cut her head off. I struck her on the head with a poker and then drew a razor across her throat.

When charged with the murder he simply replied:

Correct. I plead guilty.

Some seven weeks later, following the advice of one of those lawyers with the impossible job, he changed his plea to 'not guilty'. The case hadn't captured the imagination of the public and, surprisingly for a murder trial at the time, several seats were left vacant in the courtroom. What the local paper had once hypocritically called the 'morbid-minded' had stayed away. Their reporter, however, professionally dedicated to revealing all the gory details of the case, was present throughout the trial.

William appeared before the disappointing crowd in a dark overcoat with a velvet collar and broad check scarf. He listened attentively as his eloquent defence lawyer played his very weak hand. Defence argued that his client had served in India and suggested that he had acquired the habits of heavy drinking and a liability to be easily provoked because of his service. In brief, the army was responsible for the ex-artilleryman's short fuse.

In most such cases, the jury returned their verdict within ten minutes. Dyer's hopes must have been raised

120. Sketch of Dyer in court.

when a decision had not been after an hour. It transpired that three members had been arguing the case for manslaughter but after ninety minutes they gave way.

Traditionally, when pronouncing sentences of death the Judge concluded:

And may God have mercy on your soul.

On this occasion, the words were followed by a fervent *'Amen'* from all those present in court.

William Dyer was a dignified man and made a brief wave to a friend before being taken down. He never revealed why he murdered his sweetheart. Perhaps she had threatened to leave him once he ran out of money. Perhaps it was the combination of alcohol and his short temper. Or was it all down to the tropics?

At all events, his sole concern in prison was to meet his maker a healthy man. He worried that his sore throat would not have cleared up before the rope was placed around it. He continued to smoke and eat well, right to the end. After a breakfast of bacon and egg on his day of execution, William Dyer strode to the gallows. He did indeed *Like a soldier fall...*

Outside a hushed crowd of eight hundred people, and one morbid-minded reporter, waited silently.

FATAL STREET FIGHT·BIRMINGHAM.

A MASS OF CONTRADICTIONS

Rather than resort to the law, people in poorer areas of the city settled disputes by mixing it. Occasionally things got out of hand, resulting in serious injury or loss of life. Police turned a blind eye to minor altercations but could not look the other way when faced with a stiff on the streets.

The main problem, when cases came to court, was the unreliability of witnesses. Some could be bought at the cost of a bevvy; others lied for their own reasons, perhaps because of minor grievances against neighbours. In such scenarios it was almost impossible to know who was telling the truth and who trying to fit up an enemy.

Following a massive street brawl in a court off Lord Street in May 1912, John Edwards, a stamper and Florence Williams, a penmaker, were arrested for the murder of William Thomas Pugh.

As the case progressed, all manner of low life took to the witness stand and, after promising to tell the truth, proceeded to do the opposite.

Leah Humpage said she saw the accused Florence Williams take something bright out of the house and join in the melee. Another swore she saw John Edwards strike Pugh in the chest with the cry 'take that Billy!' A third witness stated that after the affray Edwards had confessed to him that he had hit Pugh three times with a poker.

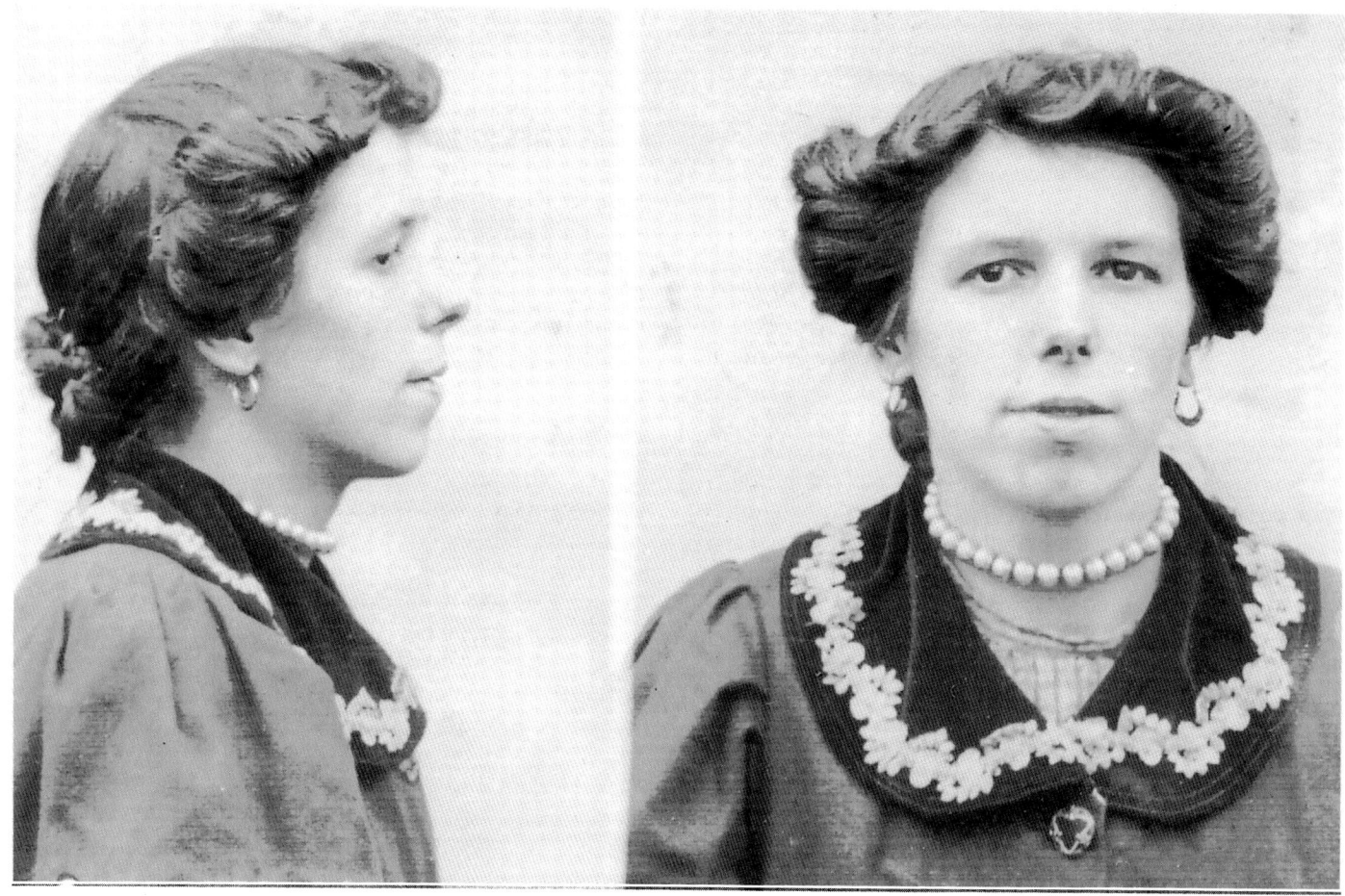

122. Florence Williams. Did she literally get away with murder?

The Judge was as confused as everyone else. In despair he said to the packed courtroom:

I have never heard such a mass of contradictions in all my life!

The jury were out for twenty minutes and not surprisingly returned with a verdict of insufficient evidence. Both Edwards and Williams were released. Someone had got away with murder. Perhaps descendants of the families still living in Birmingham know the truth?

'I FULLY INTENDED TO MURDER'

In the complex web of human relationships in Birmingham's densely populated slums 'Uncles', 'Aunts' and lodgers regularly popped into each others' homes and sometimes their beds. They would stay for weeks or months, only moving on when rent collectors started getting heavy or affairs terminated when one or both partners sobered up.

Fanny Gilligan, like most of the inhabitants of Leopold Street – one of the most squalid districts of Birmingham – led a hard life. She skivvied by day as an underpaid polisher and was regularly beaten at night by James Edward Higgins. They lived together in his mother's house. He was not technically a wife-beater as the couple were not wed to each other. In the eyes of the law, for all that counted in Leopold Street, Fanny was still married to her husband of sixteen years.

During her four year relationship with Higgins, Fanny's initial love had turned to loathing and, like many before and since, she turned to the bottle. She hated herself, her life and her partner and just lived for the few hours oblivion on tap in a public house.

On September 16th 1911, Higgins' mother purchased some paraffin for the lamp which she left in the passage leading from the kitchen. James and Fanny stumbled back from the pub around midnight. They were once again at loggerheads and more than usual the worse for wear.

James' brother returned one hour later and immediately sobered up once he inhaled the acrid smell of smoke coming from the direction of the front room. As he pulled open the door the sudden draught caught the smouldering flames, which quickly engulfed the figure slouched over the table in the middle of the room. James was being burnt alive in front of his brother's eyes. He died from horrific burns at the hospital a few hours later.

A demented Fanny was discovered cowering in the wash house, a bottle of beer in her hand, she blurted out her story to the shocked brother:

He asked me to take his boots off. Little did he think I poured a pint of lamp-oil down his legs, put a match to it and out I came.

To a neighbour who arrived to help she justified her actions:

He kicked me with his hob-nailed boot, I poured paraffin over him and set him alight.

Her statement made to police seemed a positive invitation for the hangman to pop into Winson Green on his grisly rounds:

I wilfully intended to murder that man. I poured the lamp-oil over him. I got a box of matches, lit it and set him on fire and I will do it again. Wilful murder, I meant to do it and done it. His mother fetched the lamp-oil and I poured it on him but he kicked me first. I have got my own back for my husband and myself. I do not care if I swing for it.

In the light of the above confession it became impossible to reduce the charge from murder to manslaughter.

Three months later, Fanny was tried for what became known as 'the Leopold Street Murder'. The defence argued that she was not responsible for her actions. Fanny was an epileptic and suffered several fits whilst on remand. The offence, it was argued, had been committed whilst she was having a fit aggravated by the influence of alcohol.

Dr. Brown, for the defence, argued that Fanny was insane at the time of the murder. The judge was having none of this desperate ploy.

JUDGE: *What do you mean by insane? Did she know the nature and quality of the act she was committing?*
DR. BROWN: *In my opinion no.*
JUDGE: *Her own statements show that she seems to have known all about it.*

The jury were out for thirty minutes and returned a guilty verdict with a recommendation for mercy on the grounds of provocation. When asked if she had anything to say Fanny replied:

No, I am quite willing to die but I have not done it.

Summing up the Judge argued that she had been convicted by her own mouth. When he brought up the question of mercy Fanny interrupted:

I don't want any mercy thank you.

The prisoner stood unmoved as the death sentence was passed. Before leaving the dock she revealed a terrible indictment of slum life:

I am an English woman and an Irishman's wife but prison has been my home and I am quite willing to be buried in it. I have found good friends in prison.

The death penalty was commuted to life imprisonment some three weeks later. As a result of committing murder, Fanny swapped one form of imprisonment for another but, despite the austere conditions, seemed far happier in her second life.

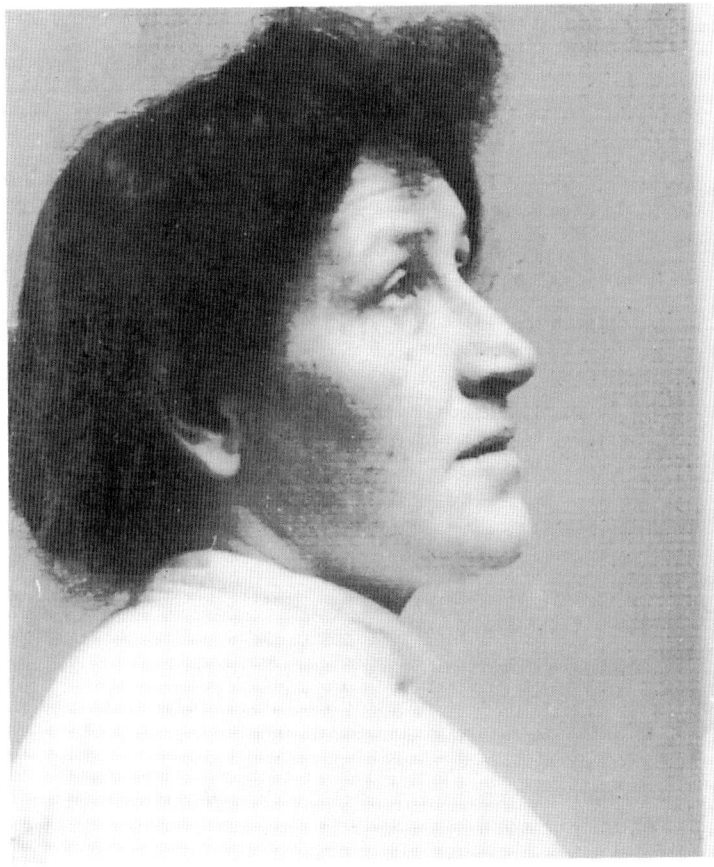
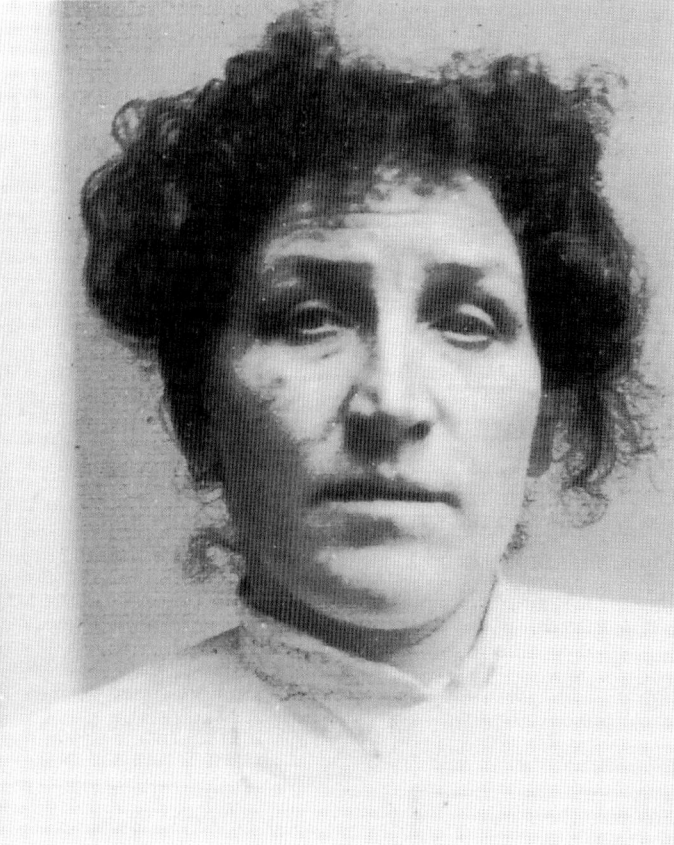

123. Fanny Gilligan poured lamp-oil over her boyfriend and set him alight in what became known as the 'Leopold Street Murder'.

LOVE ON THE DOLE

Sarah and Thomas were lovers. The only real pleasure in life for the desperately poor pair from Aston was each other's company. 17-year-old Sarah Sturdy faced a life in service, tailoring, skivvying and scrubbing floors for a few shillings. Thomas Mason, five years her senior, was unemployed, somehow scraping a living as best he could.

Seeing no future for themselves, the couple, who had been courting for a year, determined to elope. That was as far as their plans went. With no money to buy train tickets the destitute pair, hand in hand, began wandering aimlessly, looking for a new life, anything was better than the miserable existence they had endured in dwellings in Phillips Street.

They walked and they cursed the world and its injustice. Sarah pawned a dress for 2s.6d. and, it being July, the two spent their first night away from home sleeping out. The following morning Sarah pawned a ring for 1s 6d. and the couple treated themselves to the luxury of a little food in a refreshment room in Witton. A waitress later testified that she heard Thomas accuse Sarah of sleeping with somebody else.

That night the couple sought shelter in the verandah of Farnleigh cricket club in Witton. As to what happened next we have three stories, two from Mason himself and one the prosecuting counsel.

What is beyond dispute is that Sarah's body was discovered the following morning on 13th July 1911. The corpse was lying on its back, a knife protruding from the left breast. Her blouse had been pulled up from the waist and the knife thrust into the flesh. At no time did the weapon pass through her clothes. One of her hands gripped her skirt.

Two days later Thomas surrendered to a policeman on Colmore Row. The surprised bobby made notes as the scruffy young man blurted out his story:

> *You had better take me to the police station for murdering the girl at Witton on Tuesday. I left the knife in her but her screams frightened me so I walked out or else I should have done myself in. I have walked about since and I am tired out.*

When his mother visited him in gaol she pulled no punches. *'Did you do it?'* Thomas once again confessed to the murder but when the case came to court he pleaded 'not guilty', retracting his confessions, saying that at the time he made them he had wanted to die.

In a statement to police, which he stuck to in court, Thomas said that both he and Sarah had made a suicide pact and agreed to die together. He added that Sarah had held the knife against her breast with one hand and pressed it home with the other. According to Thomas the dying girl groaned terribly, raised her head and kissed him one last time.

Doubt was swiftly cast over this romanticised version of events by prosecution witnesses. A doctor argued that the knife, which Thomas had stolen from his home, had been thrust into the girl's breast right up to the handle. Sarah was probably sitting when the fatal wound was inflicted. He argued that it was extremely improbable that she could have caused the wounds herself and death would have resulted within thirty seconds.

The jury returned at 7.12pm and no sooner had they entered the jury box than the electric lights in the court went out. Thomas Mason was found guilty with a recommendation to mercy. He insisted they were wrong:

> *I have not done it!*

Mason was the first prisoner for many years to be sentenced to death by candle-light. The recommendation to mercy was acted upon and the sentence reduced to life imprisonment.

THE MURDER OF BIRMINGHAM LIZZIE

By the age of 34, Frank Greening was ready to settle down. The housepainter wrote to an old flame, Elizabeth Hearne – then living in London as 'Birmingham Lizzie' – and invited her back to her roots.

In February 1913 Lizzie disembarked at New Street and made for the Gooch Street district where the re-united couple set up home. They were to move several times over the next two months. The old saying about not knowing someone until you lived with them certainly applied to Frank and Lizzie. Almost from day one their neighbours' peace was disrupted by violent slanging matches between the incompatible pair. Lizzie quickly tired of the relationship and moved to 5, Bissell Street. On Sunday April 7th, the bad penny turned up. Following a brief conversation, Frank put his hand in his jacket pocket, produced a revolver and pumped three bullets into his former partner. Then, pulling his hat over his eyes and turning his collar up, Greening strode off with a brisk step across the yard.

The following day, in hospital barely clinging to life, Lizzie was told she had a visitor, a man claiming to be a relative. It was Greening, who had the audacity to visit the woman he had shot to beg her to drop the charges!

Lizzie was in no position to drop anything, succumbing to her injuries hours later.

On Wednesday August 13th 1913 Greening was the first man to be executed at Winson Green in nine years. Having no intention of making his peace with God, he spent a restless night on the eve of his execution, showering his prison attendants with torrents of foul-mouthed abuse. He received the ministrations of the chaplain churlishly and went to the scaffold still abusing his captors.

CANAL, CUT-THROAT OR CARBOLIC?

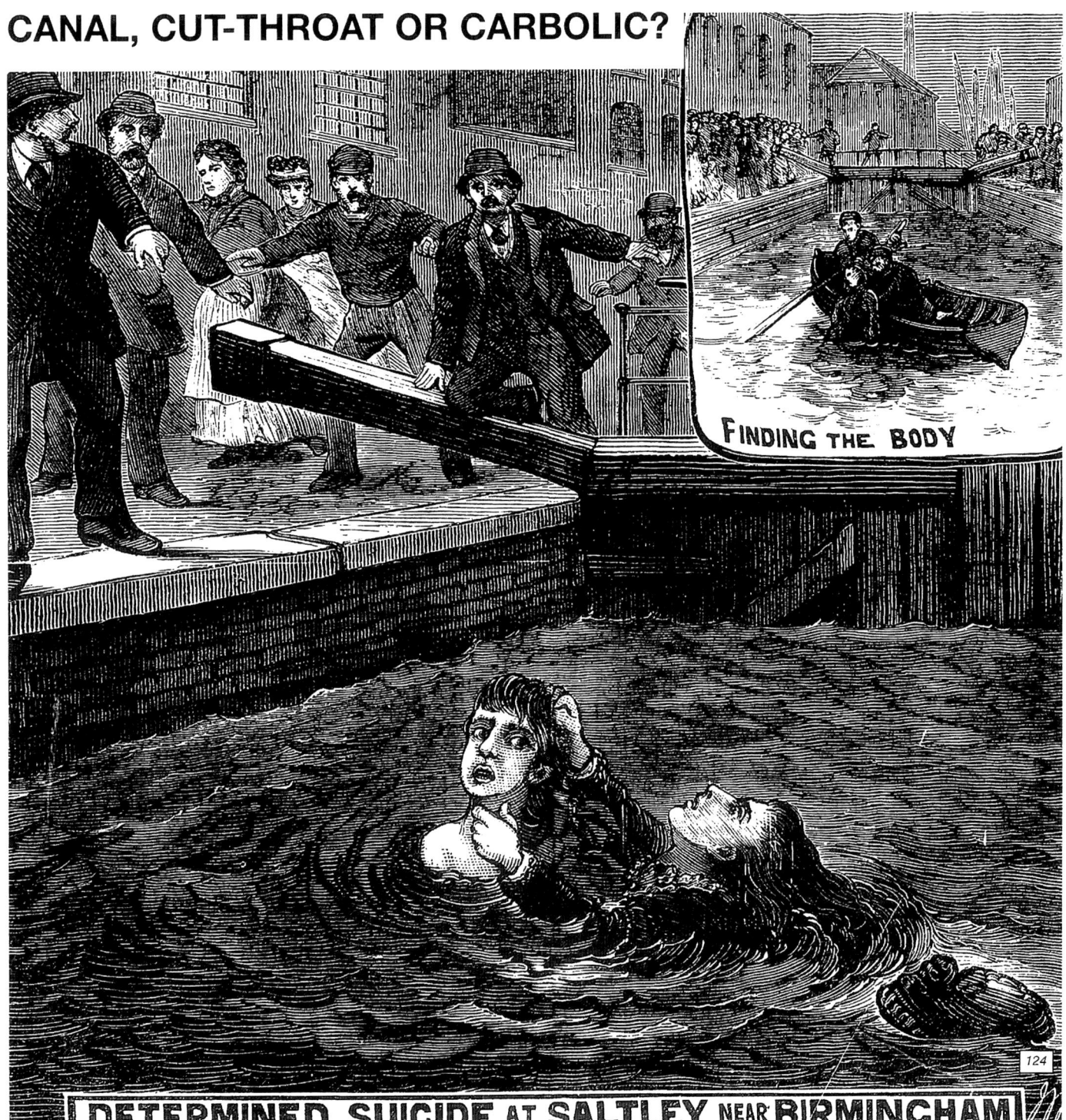

Newspapers ran hundreds of stories of successful and unsuccessful suicide attempts, many centred on canals. The *Illustrated Police News* picked up one of the cases which it published in May 1886 under the headline:

DETERMINED SUICIDE AT SALTLEY

There was a report in Birmingham's Post of the finding of a body of a girl in the canal locks, near Landor Street, late on the previous evening. Further inquiry reveals the fact that the deceased committed suicide in a most determined manner. Her named is Emma Salmon and she is 18 years of age, and has been lodging at 20, Vauxhall Road. It appears that a young man named Leek, who lives in Garrison-lane, was walking along the towing-path of the Birmingham and Warwick Junction Canal, near Landor-street, shortly before eleven o'clock on Monday, when he heard a noise in the canal. On looking into the locks he observed a young woman in the water. Stripping himself of his clothing he gallantly plunged in to the rescue. The girl, however, desperately resisted his efforts to save her from drowning. Clutching him by the throat she held on to him until he was almost choked, and to save himself he was at last compelled to release his hold, and to swim out of the lock to the towing-path, where he was taken from the water in an almost exhausted condition. So desperate had been the efforts of the young woman to resist the endeavours made to save her that it was noticed afterwards that his neck and face bore marks of violence.

A great crowd had by this time assembled, and the greatest excitement prevailed. A search for the body of the girl was then made, and it was discovered by a boatman named Wilkins, with the help of other persons.

*Once I was happy, but now I am forlorn,
Like an old coat that's ragged and torn,
No one to care for me, through the wide world
I roam.*

These words, written on a tatty scrap of paper found beside a pond in Castle Bromwich, were Mary Turner's last communication with the living world. Her tale was as old and tragic as time itself – boy meets girl – girl falls pregnant – boy leaves girl. The story is so common today that few people are surprised or shocked by such a course of events but attitudes were so very different in the nineteenth century, and indeed first half of the twentieth.

Mary Ann Turner, a dressmaker employed at the Warwick House, Birmingham, had been stepping out with William Bagnall, the son of a brickmaker living at Hodge Hill, some five miles from the city. Following his proposal of marriage, the couple determined to get to

THE SUICIDE.

know each other a little more intimately. When Mary told William she was pregnant he arranged to speed up proceedings so their child would not be in evidence at the wedding ceremony. The young man's father, however, for reasons best known to himself, urged his son to wait a few more weeks before tying the knot.

Following a heated row over the pregnancy with her stepmother, Mary was thrown out penniless onto the streets. There was only one place to go. The distraught young woman sought shelter, relief and sympathy at the home of her future husband. She was in for a rude awakening. Knocking on the door in Hodge Hill, Mary was confronted by the stubborn Bagnall senior, who was adamant that there was no room at the inn.

In desperation Mary fled to the church where her lover, Bagnall junior, was rehearsing with the choir. William had had a change of heart: having had his fun, he had no intention of facing up to his responsibilities. After a few blunt home truths he adjourned to the Barley Mow public house to ponder his problem over a pint.

Mary fretted outside. William quaffed within.

As he left the pub, the by now hysterical mother-to-be seized hold of his arm and beseeched him to take her home:

Will, I have no work, no money and no bed to sleep on.

Will, strengthened by alcohol-induced courage, stood his ground. Even though he knew Mary had been thrown out on her ear he insisted that she return home. He refused to give her any money. Mary played her last desperate card, threatening to destroy herself if he would not care for her.

SMOKING RUINS OF BARN—BAGNALLS HOUSE IN DISTANCE

Will walked away. Mary walked to the pond.
Will prepared his meal. Mary prepared herself.
Will went to bed. Mary went to sleep.

The body was discovered floating in the pond the following morning.

At inquest, when Mary's last words were read out and the full heartlessness of the Bagnalls was revealed, a vast wave of outrage and indignation swept over the people of Birmingham.

Threatening letters were sent to the father and son and for several days their home was almost permanently in a state of siege. The Bagnall's dared not show themselves and food had to be smuggled in by friends.

On a Sunday morning in March 1886 their house was raided by 'thousands of Birmingham roughs' who quickly overpowered the inadequate force of twenty policemen guarding the premises. The assault developed into a full-scale riot of looting and made the front page of the *Illustrated Police News*:

SCENE AT THE BACK OF HOUSE

In the afternoon the "rough" contingent from Birmingham, Saltley, and other districts commenced operations by breaking the fences and hurling showers of stones at the house. Every pane of glass was broken, and the window frames were torn away. The roughs then broke into the house through the roof of the kitchen, which is a low structure and possessed themselves of many of the contents.

They pitched out to their comrades bread, meat, butter and eggs and followed this up by throwing outside saucepans, kettles, and every other culinary utensil they could lay their hands on. They also seized a beer barrel, and rolled it out of doors down a steep hill into the crowd.

Afterwards a heavy wagon was taken from the outbuildings and that was also rolled down the hill, together with a light spring cart and some of the machinery from the brickworks...The mob then gathered the debris of woodwork into a vast pile, and setting fire to it, created a conflagration which could be seen for miles around.

During the attack on the kitchen part of the roof fell on one of Bagnall's daughters, and so seriously injured her that she had to be taken in a cab to one of the Birmingham hospitals.

MOB ATTACKING FRONT OF BAGNALLS HOUSE

The father and son, the initial targets of the mob, had previously fled, and if they valued their lives, such was the power of the people, they were probably not seen in the area again.

131. Sarah and William passed along Moseley Road minutes before her final fling.

Famously having more canals than Venice, Birmingham poses a dilemma to its suicidal: where to go for their final fling. Without witnesses, proving whether a drowning was accident, suicide or murder was extremely difficult. The jury at the coroner's court in June 1883 faced just such a problem.

William Emery stood accused of drowning seventeen-year-old Sarah Davies whose body was found in the Birmingham and Fazeley canal, near Garrison-lane. The jury listened attentively to accounts of the deeply depressed domestic's last hours.

Emily Preston, who had known Sarah for several months, told the hushed court that her friend had recently been very depressed, not wanting to take up a job in service which her father had recently arranged for her. On the eve of her demise the two teenagers met at 8.40 pm. Sarah was accompanied by a young man Emily had never seen before. She appeared to be in good spirits, as if a weight had been taken off her mind. Had she determined on a final course of action which would solve all her problems? The conversation certainly seems to support the theory:

EMILY: *Well Sarah, we have met again.*
SARAH: *Yes, for the last time.*
EMILY: *When are you leaving?*
SARAH: *You will know very soon.*

Sarah then added that she was going to see her mother, but it would be for the last time. She then wandered off with the young man and was never seen alive again.

Dr. Barratt, who made the post-mortem examination, was next to give evidence. He testified that the girl had died from drowning, there being no external marks of violence.

Finally William Emery, accused on no evidence whatsoever, was asked his side of the story. The young man stated that he met Sarah for the first time just after 7.30 pm on the night she died. The couple, eating nuts and fruit, wandered around aimlessly for several hours. Late in the evening Sarah seemed to have a destination in mind. Slotting her arm through his, Sarah drew Emery from the bench in the park near Moseley Road, onto Bradford Street, through Dale End, and Lawley Street and onto Landor Street. Arriving at the canal bridge, Sarah suggested they part:

You go home: I am not going back this way.

With the hour being so late, it was now past midnight, William insisted that his new friend should not go home alone. The couple linked arms again and strolled along the canal, both sober, both chattering pleasantly.

Suddenly, with no warning whatsoever, Sarah, who was closest to the canal, jumped in it, dragging her shocked partner with her into the filthy water. Emery continued his testimony:

She loosed me as soon as she got into the water, and plunged into the middle of the canal before I could take hold of her. I scrambled out and ran across the waste ground into Garrison-lane and then to Great Barr Street.

When asked why he had not tried to save Sarah, Emery replied that he could not swim. The only detectable flaw in the young man's story was that, when he found a policeman, some ten minutes after scrambling out of the canal, he had been walking, not running.

After fifty minutes of deliberation, the jury found that Sarah had died from drowning, but that there was insufficient evidence as to how she got into the water.

Along with canal water, overdoses of laudanum or iodine were gulped down with regular frequency and the aptly named cut-throat razor put to its literal use. Then as now, many more men than women succeeded in their quest for self-destruction. Those whose attempts were unsuccessful listed a variety of reasons for attempting suicide. In 1897 15-year-old Minnie Ewer of Lawley Street jumped into the canal because her sister called her 'bad names'. Kate McDonnagh drank iodine as she was afraid of an impending operation. David Crump, a 48-year-old labourer, was remanded for a week on a charge of attempting to commit suicide. He claimed to have abandoned his attempt *upon discovering that steel hurt.*

Sometimes those considered still at risk were remanded, detained in hospital or discharged to the care of their parents. Some just kept on trying while others just couldn't get anything right. Perhaps 'Look before you leap' would have been an appropriate headline to the following snippet, which appeared in the newspaper on March 17th, 1900:

Henry Cundy, carter of 67, Lichfield Road, Aston, who has been remanded twice previously on a charge of attempting suicide, was now committed to the asylum. He jumped off Salford Bridge, Graveley Hill, on 3rd. March, 1900, but landed on the footpath instead of in the water.

132. Did she jump or was she pushed? In 1883 William Emery was charged with the murder of Sarah Davies whose body was found in the Birmingham and Fazeley canal. The court accepted the young man's story that Sarah had suddenly jumped into the water and pulled him in with her.

133. The Old Worcester Wharf. Canals were handy for both the murderous and suicidal.

In July 1901 Henry Edward Robeson, who had suffered from gout for 27 years, hanged himself. He left a note on the kitchen table:

Forgive me all; I am mad, mad, mad!

Herbert Allen was as equally hell bent on self-destruction, but he had no intention of dying lonely. If you have no fear of death then why not take an enemy along with you? Following his dismissal as a barman in Temple street in 1896 Allen returned and casually shot his former employer, Henry Skinner.

At the trial the defence argued a plea of temporary insanity, saying suicide ran in the family – Allen's two brothers and his father had all shot themselves, though only one brother had died. Found guilty, Allen made one of the most bizarre speeches ever heard following sentence of death. It concluded:

It has been my hope and certainty that you would condemn me. That alone has been the means of restraining me from committing suicide whilst in prison...I bought a revolver and cartridges even at the age of twelve, but my father took them from me, and I have tried other ways to get rid of myself. But that does not matter now, as you are going to do it for me, and I am pleased that I shall not commit suicide after all. I sincerely thank everyone for their kind sympathy, and trust that they will not petition the Government for a reprieve for me, as I should only strangle myself the first opportunity if you obtain one.

Either some sort of reprieve came through or Herbert took up DIY as there is no record of his execution.

We too come to an end to this journey back in time to the darker side of life and death in Victorian and Edwardian Birmingham. If you enjoyed reading the book half as much as I did researching and writing it, I'm sure you've had a wicked read. If any mistakes have inadvertently been included, or if you've spotted photos of your ancestors, please drop me a line so I may include the information if/when the book is reprinted.

STEVE JONES, SEPTEMBER, 1998

ACKNOWLEDGEMENTS

My main thanks must go to Dave Cross, the curator of the excellent West Midlands Police Museum. He is an excellent raconteur, extremely enthusiastic about police and criminal history, and, most importantly, knows his stuff!

As may be witnessed by the illustration acknowledgements most of the photos are from the West Midlands Police Museum which I would highly recommend. There's something there to interest everyone - school pupil and research graduate, police and public.

Birmingham Central Library is a credit to the city. It's well-stocked, spacious and teamed by enthusiastic and knowledgeable staff only too willing to answer my sometimes sinister questions.

Last but not least I would like to thank Viv Foster. We have our annual war of words as she tidies up the text whilst telling me off for being vague and lazy. The text flows much more smoothly once cut, pasted and edited by a professional.

STEVE JONES 1998

ILLUSTRATION ACKNOWLEDGEMENTS

West Midlands Police Museum:
9, 13, 15, 16, 17, 33, 37, 38, 55, 59, 61, 62, 63, 68, 74, 75, 77, 79, 80, 82, 84, 85, 86, 87, 88, 89, 94, 95, 97, 98, 99, 103, 107, 108, 109, 110, 114, 115, 122, 123.

Birmingham Library Services:
1, 2, 3, 4, 5, 6, 7, 8, 18, 20, 21, 22, 23, 27, 29, 30, 34, 35, 78, 81, 131, 133.

Warwickshire County Record Office:
12, 14, 48, 49, 51, 53, 54, 56, 57, 58, 64, 96, 104.

The Public Record Office:
10, 24, 25, 31, 40, 41, 42, 43, 44, 45, 46, 47, 50, 52, 60, 66, 90, 91, 92, 93, 100, 101, 102, 105, 106, 111.

Also Available ...

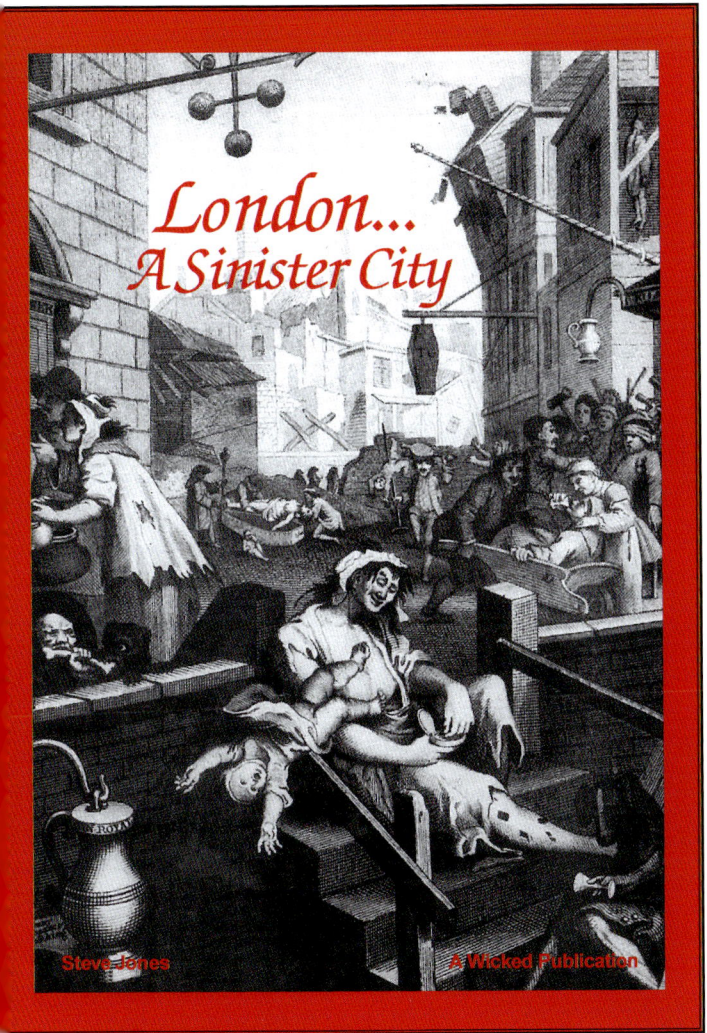

An examination of the darker side of London's history in an alternative guide to the capital.
First hand accounts of public hangings where thousands were strung up before vast crowds as a deterrent in the days before an effective police force. The executions induced a carnival-like atmosphere. Princes and paupers were not treated identically - the rich, royal and religious were beheaded and burned.
Chapters include 'Sex and the City', 'Jack the Ripper' and 'Bring Out Your Dead' which examine the beastial living conditions and crimes experienced by the majority of Londoners. Much use is made of contemporary accounts and stark uncensored photographs and illustrations.

ISBN 978-1-84491-887-4
£19.99

Visit the West Midlands Police Museum at the Steelhouse Lane Lock-up: check **www.WMPeelers.com** for details of events and further information about the history of policing in the West Midlands

Lock-up Sketch by Eric Cook Jan 2018